HR for SMEs

3-steps to building

your Human Resources

foundation

BY PAULA FISHER

Cover design: Leah Nicholas

Published by Pearl Escapes on behalf of Practical HR

Practical HR Ltd.

PHR House

34b Star Lane,

Great Wakering

Essex, SS3 0FF

www.practicalhr.co.uk

www.yourhr.space

Printed in Great Britain by Bell & Bain Ltd, Glasgow

For every business leader

who has ever felt overwhelmed

or held back by HR

and employment law

Contents

Introduction – Who This Book Is for and How to Use It

This book is predominately for business owners and directors of SMEs (small to medium sized enterprises) who are responsible for HR (Human Resources) decisions in the business. They may be supported by a PA, office manager or someone in finance and in 'medium sized' organisations there may be an official HR department, so this book will also benefit anyone else in the organisation who is *doing* the day-to-day HR management, but throughout the book I'll be talking to you as though you are the actual business owner or director of an SME, so, hello!

This book will provide you with a guide to help you make HR management more effective, and throughout the book I'll demonstrate how the right HR systems can add value. It will show you how effective HR processes can actually support your business and contribute positively to its growth. And, how the right HR foundation can make your life easier and even save you money! This book also aims to help you remove some of the frustration that can come with HR confusion!

When you are in control of your HR framework (rather than feeling out of control), you can achieve great things with your people. This helps you move your business forward with confidence.

This book promotes the concept that you need to have a solid HR foundation in place that will support the business as it grows. It's a bit like building a house. You would not build a house without foundations, and you should not employ people without solid HR foundations.

There is a view held by many people that employment law (and hence HR) is all on the side of the employee, and that the business is powerless to act. I do NOT share this view, and I hope to demonstrate this as you read on. If you have the right foundation in place and do things in the right way, employment law will support the business and allow you to make the commercial decisions you may have to make in any situation. Ultimately your strong HR foundation should support managerial prerogative.

In this book I'll identify what makes up the HR foundation and how to make sure it is robust and can support the business, discussing case studies and giving recommendations.

With the foundation in place, you can then build on it, and I will discuss some additional areas that can further support your business.

This book is not a pink and fluffy HR book! It recognises that HR management must add value. It needs to be in tune with the commercial needs of the business. With good HR systems in place you will have the confidence to make the HR decisions you need to make for your business, and let's face it, sometimes these decisions are difficult and even a bit scary! Please do not think that I'm talking about being an onerous or unfair employer. To the contrary, to achieve a solid HR foundation and beyond you need to employ good HR practices as it is all about getting the most out of your people for everyone's benefit (including theirs!)

From a personal perspective, I don't want any SME to be held back because of poor HR planning. I don't want business owners to be held back from making the commercial decisions that are needed for their business because they are frightened of HR fallout or being on the wrong side of employment law. That's not good for your business and it's not good for the majority of people who work in your business.

So how should you use this book?

The best way to use this book is to read it from start to end.

As explained above, this book promotes getting a solid HR foundation in place and my 3-step guide is summarised in Chapter 2, with much more detail and the 'how to' in Chapters 4, 5 and 6.

If you want to just 'dip-in' to topics that are of interest, start with Chapter 1 and then dip-in to the chapters you like the sound of! Hopefully, dipping-in will then encourage you to read other chapters or the whole book.

If you are a business owner, I know you didn't start your business to become a HR manager! But it's one of the things that come with running a successful business. Your HR foundation is like many other areas of your business; once it's in place, it will run more smoothly and take up less of your time. It will need some ongoing maintenance, but it will support your business as it grows.

Terms and information

Some terms and information related to this book:

SME

As I mentioned, this book is predominantly for SMEs. SME stands for **small to medium sized enterprise**. The government's definition is an organisation that employs between five and 250 employees. Those with less than five employees are normally referred to as micro businesses, those with more than 250 employees, as large businesses.

HR

Stands for Human Resources and this term is used throughout the book. Sometimes I refer to the function itself, other times to those who are responsible for HR within an organisation. The problem with HR is that it is a very broad (almost umbrella) term covering just about every topic that relates to people within an organisation – from recruitment, payroll, benefits, employment law, training, appraisals, employee relations, administration etc. So I will try to be clear about which area I'm talking about at any time – but sometimes I will use it as an umbrella term!

Employment Law

This is not intended to be an employment law book. However, you cannot talk about HR without reference to employment law and employment regulations. Indeed, these are key areas that those who look after any aspect of HR need to get to grips with (or have some support to get to grips with) if they are to be effective in managing HR and putting in a solid HR foundation. The law that I do mention is based wholly on UK law. I hope to show you throughout this book how employment law can support an organisation and that it does not have to be so scary or hold a business back.

Football

Throughout this book I use football analogies! It's not that I'm a football fan (so don't worry if you're not), it could be any sport. The purpose is to help you look at HR from another perspective and to show that it's not the 'black art' you may think it is!

Free Resources

There are a number of free resources mentioned throughout the book. These include checklists, example policy document and general information. There is a full list at the back and details of how you can access these.

Chapter 1 – The Human Resources Game

Red tape... compliance... ticking boxes... costly... time consuming... frustrating ...not my job!

Be honest, when you think about HR in your business, are these the kind of phrases that first spring to mind? Is HR a game you don't want to play?

Let's just admit it. HR has developed a negative image. Rather than a help, it is often seen as a hindrance and a necessary evil! It's about bureaucracy and red tape. It's about what you **cannot** do rather than what you can do, and is seen as being at odds with the commercial needs of the business!

The trouble is that, if you are running any kind of business that employs people, this means *doing* HR. In fact, every small to medium sized enterprise (SME) *does* HR, they may just call it a different name. And may not do it as well as they could!

If you ask any small business owner what frustrates them in their company, most will include HR and talk about problems with their staff. They will tell you about people who fail to do what they're supposed to do or what they say they will do! They will complain that people 'let them down' or take advantage. This is what they relate HR with... and blame HR for!

However, HR does not have to be like this.

Imagine your people worked and performed to the standard you wanted them to and with care and commitment. Imagine people did not let you down or take advantage but got on with the job at hand and worked together to contribute to the needs of the business. Would that make your life easier? Would that add value to your business? Would it free up your time so you could concentrate on other aspects of your business? Well, this is what this book is all about... so read on!

What we need to remember is that HR is about people and, if there's one thing you can guarantee, it's the fact that people will be unpredictable, and they are all different. We all have our own agendas, priorities, strengths and weaknesses, skills, likes and dislikes. You cannot change this fact, but, for the business owner who puts their heart and soul into the company and expects their employees to do the same (but doesn't always see it happening), people can be infuriating.

The only way through these frustrations is to tackle HR head-on and accept that this is part of running a successful business.

But here comes the next woe – the legal complications!

All the processes involved in employing people, from recruitment to contracts of employment, performance management to disciplinary procedures, all seem to come with the burden of ever-increasing and ever-changing employment regulation. And the one thing that is a certainty is that employment law is always changing.

The result is that handling HR in SMEs is usually approached with a kind of intrinsic fear – the fear of saying the wrong thing, doing the wrong thing, mismanaging a sticky situation or winding up in an employment tribunal. Because of this, often people just do nothing!

Adding to this problem is the fact that most SMEs will not have, and financially cannot justify having, a dedicated, experienced HR professional. So, business owners and managers in SMEs must get involved in HR management every day. They have no choice as they cannot tell an employee to 'go talk to' HR or call up the HR Department to 'sort out a problem'. (Even those SMEs that do have an HR department or use an external HR company actually still 'do' HR on a day to day basis as they will still be managing people).

But, being driven by fear and having limited in-house expertise makes SMEs more vulnerable as it's all too easy for them to unknowingly fall foul of the law.

If all of this wasn't enough to put people off, the HR world seems to have been infected with a nasty virus which has the unfortunate symptom of generating confusing jargon or 'HR speak'.

Consider a few examples:

- Competencies
- Onboarding
- Emotional intelligence
- Redeployment
- Workforce optimisation

Realistically, how much do any of us truly understand these terms?

Even the HR Department's name has been infected. Where once it was Personnel, it is now Human Resources or... wait for it... Talent Management... and even HR Capital. I'm sure some people have come up with other suggestions; Human Remains was suggested by one client!

With this lack of understanding, fear about the legal implications, confusing jargon and endless frustrations over how to manage people, is it any wonder that most people running small to medium sized businesses consider human resource management to be a complete minefield – something to be avoided at all cost?

However, despite the obstacles, SMEs must still get a grip on HR. So how do they do that?

Basic considerations

To start with, HR within an SME must be appropriate for the size of the organisation. It cannot be the same as HR in a large corporate organisation. It must be **practical and have a commercial focus** that is in tune with the needs of the business (actually HR in the corporate world should also be practical and have a commercial focus – but that's a discussion for another time). Suffice to say, the SME manager who 'copies' HR policy documents from their last corporate employer and thinks these are appropriate will be tying themselves in knots and doing more harm than good!

HR is not only about staying on the right side of the law. Yes, there is red tape and every business owner should act as a responsible and lawful employer. Indeed, if you get your foundation right, the law can support your business and give you the flexibility you need. But, the purpose of HR in any business goes further than this. Think about the actual term 'human resource' for a moment. Just like any other resource you have in your organisation there are basic practical questions you need to ask about it:

- How much of this resource do you need?
- How much can you afford?
- How can you get the most out of this resource?

I'm aware this sounds a bit 'cold' and impersonal but, in business, employing and managing people comes with a commercial reality. At its very basic level, you need to be able to afford to pay and train the people you employ and get a return on your investment!

As an SME, with limited resources at your disposal, this is even more important. With far fewer people than your corporate equivalent, the percentage of 'contribution per person' for an SME is much higher. Everyone in a small business has to add value and so it is crucial that they know what is required of them. It's a bit like playing 5-a-side football – each player has a lot more ground to cover so if one player is 'off their game' the impact on the team is much greater.

So, your employees are potentially both one of your biggest liabilities and one of your greatest assets. The liabilities come from all angles – everything from the underperforming member of staff to employment law and the employee who decides to sue you. The strength that your team can bring to the organisation, however, comes when you witness great performance and dedication towards achieving the goals of the business. Effective HR can help you avoid or deal with the potential liabilities and achieve the best possible business outcomes through your people.

In other words, **your people are your business** and, through effective or ineffective HR and management of those people, you'll either succeed together or fail together.

In the early stages of building up a business, the HR function often focused on the pure essentials – maybe setting up an employee file, running payroll and having a basic offer letter in place... and some policies you copied from a previous company! However, as your organisation grows, it's important to see how your HR management actually integrates with and impacts your entire business. This is why it is so important that it is aligned to the needs of your business and that you get the HR foundation right.

So, it's time to move away from thinking of HR as the necessary evil that keeps you out of court and start seeing its true value.

A more purposeful way of looking at HR is to see it as your means of equipping your business with the people it needs to achieve its aims. Of managing and developing those people with a long-term approach to achieving your business goals.

Looking at it this way will make HR more effective and will give your business the commercial advantage that comes with creating value through people.

Simple right?

Well, I can't pretend it isn't a bit more complex, but please believe me when I say that making HR an integral part of your business doesn't have to be overly complicated.

Good HR can make running your business easier and more productive, give you a competitive edge, save you time and money and help you sleep at night! Good HR can help you enjoy your business more than you may do now!

Before we get into any kind of detail though, let me give you an analogy to help explain the purpose of HR in any business... so let's talk about football!

What has HR got to do with football?

To be honest we could be talking about any team sport, but I've chosen football as it is probably the most popular.

So... imagine your business is a game of football.

You recruit a new player who previously played rugby. You can see they have many transferable skills that they can bring to your team. But imagine this new player has never heard of football before. (Unlikely I know, but go with me).

Your new player goes out on the pitch and the first thing they do is pick up the ball and run with it. They are immediately given a red card and sent off!

That's what we can do with new people when they join our business! We don't tell them the rules and how we play our game. We don't 'induct' them properly and then we get annoyed when they break the rules or don't do as we wanted them to!

Football plays such a big part of popular culture that I'm sure you could ask almost anyone if they knew the rules and they would say yes – perhaps with the exception of the off-side rule! We take it for granted that we know what it's all about but, when you think about it, you haven't always known how the game is played. At some point (at school, watching TV, playing with friends) you had to learn the rules.

Business owners can be guilty of thinking that everyone knows the rules of their business (as well as they know football). The truth is they won't. The business owner has been living, sleeping and breathing their business so they know what they mean. They know their own rules (especially the unwritten ones!) and 'assume' that staff will also know and understand them. **One of the biggest roles HR has to play is to ensure that there is clarity around the rules (and standards) of the business.**

Setting rules and standards also means that you have to communicate them in a way that everyone understands. And, even when everyone knows the rules, you still need a referee to enforce them.

In football, every player on the pitch knows their position, the job they have to do and the value it adds to the team. They also know the consequences of moving out of position! The last thing you need is a goalie that decides to sprint up the other end of the pitch to try to score a goal!

In business terms they have job descriptions and performance indicators and the business has communicated what the business is aiming for – its plan and goals.

In football each team has to have established what league they are playing in (or want to play in). They may be aiming for the Premier League or they might be happy playing in a Sunday league. Their overall goal or plan will affect the decisions they make about the players they recruit, the training regime and the overall standards of the team.

In business terms, as the owner you will know the goals and aims for the business and you will need people to help you realise those aims. So…

- What skills and experience do you want people to have?
- How do you want people to behave and conduct themselves?
- What standards and rules do you have?
- How do you want things done?
- Are these written down and communicated clearly?
- Are you enforcing your rules and are there consequences if rules are broken?
- How do you help new people settle into the company and contribute quickly?
- How do you develop people and their skills?

- How do you deal with people who want to (or have to) leave the business?
- Does everyone know their role and how they contribute to the overall business plan?
- If it all goes wrong, where does the buck stop?

In a nutshell, all of this is HR or impacts on HR!

OK, I'd like you to just quickly take another look at that last question because this is really the sting in the tail. The responsibility for HR in an SME will ultimately stop with the business owner, even if they are not *doing* the day-to-day HR management.

When things go wrong in a game of football, the fans rarely turn on their favourite player. No, the manager is the first to be called into question. They are the ones who are ultimately responsible because they have made the key decisions about the game plan and the players.

It's the same in your business. If your team is not 'playing' well, it's ultimately down to you. It's **your business** and **your responsibility.** You ultimately decide who to employ and who to keep in your business (save for people resigning). This means having to make some tough decisions along the way about people.

Being a 'nice' employer

There is not a single company that I have worked with, who set out to be a bad employer. However, in the attempt to be a good employer, many have found that 'being nice' has backfired and that, without the HR foundation in place to protect themselves or deal with situations correctly, they are taken advantage of or some kind of conflict arises.

Very simply, you cannot be a nice employer until you have the proper HR foundation in place!

I believe that the vast majority of people want to go to work and do a good job, they want to feel that they belong, get a sense of satisfaction, feel appreciated and valued, as well as receiving some recognition for the contribution they have made. Who wouldn't want this?

However, there will always be individuals who do **not** want to do a good job: the minority whose agendas are more around being disruptive, negative, complaining and doing as little as possible. You don't want these people on your team or in your business.

Then there are people who want to do a good job, but are either out of their depth, have not had the training or support, or are just not capable of doing the job that you need them to do.

It is down to you to protect your business against the minority, dealing with them quickly and effectively and exiting them from your business (or not recruiting them in the first place). To train those who want to perform or help them to move on positively if they are not capable. And to support, encourage and develop everyone who is working with you.

The key to doing this is putting the foundation in place and processes that will help you test, measure and realise whether people are doing what they should/need to be doing or not. This allows you to be objective about such matters and help manage your employees' expectations. When necessary, this will also help you with exiting people from the business.

In this book I'm going to show you a practical approach to do just this, and ensure a harmonious relationship between you, your business objectives and your people.

If you have some kind of HR support already (in-house or external), this book should also help you give it a health check:

- Is it providing your business with the foundation it needs to be protected and flexible?
- Is it helping you to manage and find solutions to any given situation as it arises?
- Is it aligned to your overall aims for the business?
- Is it adding value and allowing you to move your business forward with confidence?
- And are you actually allowing your in-house or external HR provider to add value or do you just want them to be reactive and do the basics?

Getting your HR foundation right will not only help you avoid the pitfalls, but also ensure your people work for you and impact on your business in the most positive way.

A client said something to me recently that I think really drives this point home:

"Having a problem employee makes you never want to employ anyone again. Having a great team makes you feel as if you can take on the world!"

IMPORTANT NOTE

References in this book are made to UK employment law only: but as a practical guide there are plenty of general principles and ideas that you can apply to your business, wherever in the world you might be operating.

Chapter 2 – The HR Foundation

In any game you need rules. A game of football would not be the same if there were no clear rules (and consequences to breaking those rules).

It's the same with any sport. It needs to be the same in any business.

In your business you decide what rules and standards you want. In this chapter, we discuss how.

If your house did not have solid foundations, things would start to fall apart and you would continually be making repairs. This would be time consuming and costly, not to say frustrating. You would not have the time or the money to get on with the other things in your home.

It's the same with HR. Without that foundation, you will continually be distracted from growing and developing your business as your time is taken up with interruptions, poor conduct or performance situations, or general people 'issues'.

But with this in place, you will be able to set clear boundaries and have the protection and flexibility you need as a business, which in turn will allow you to move on and develop other areas of your business, including supporting your people to work to their fullest potential (which we will discuss later).

Your foundation includes setting out the key standards and rules you want in your business. How you want to do things and how you want things to be done. This will directly influence the culture and the 'feeling' in your business. So, a solid foundation will reinforce what's important to you.

However, a poor foundation (or no foundation!) can mean that you are unwittingly diluting your values, culture and standards. Before you know it, it doesn't feel like your business anymore, as things are not being done in the way you want and it no longer reflects what's important to you.

As well as your standards, your rules and how you want things to be done, the foundation includes some legal stuff to give you protection and flexibility.

People who look after HR are often criticised for not being commercially aware or out of sync with the rest of the business. If this happens then HR cannot fulfil its purpose, which, in a nutshell is about helping the business achieve its commercial objectives through people. This means that HR is about getting the **right people** with the **right skills** in the **right place** (with the right attitude) at the **right time**!

HR should not and cannot operate in isolation of the needs of the business, as otherwise it will not add value and *will* be seen as a hindrance and not a help!

For HR to achieve its purpose, those responsible need to be clear about the business plan, the commercial needs of the business and employ the right HR practices to support them.

It is a big problem if those responsible for HR just do not 'get it' when it comes to the commercial (and legal) needs of the business. They want to be nice and avoid making difficult decisions. They do not understand the rationale for having certain contractual terms... so they don't include them. They draft bureaucratic procedures and/or policies that do not support the business. All without understanding the potential impact this can have on the business.

A more commercial approach is to have comprehensive terms that protect the business and give it options in any situation; policies that support the culture as well as meeting legal requirements; and rules and standards that reflect and support the current position, values and needs of the business.

It can also be the case that those looking after HR feel conflicted and are not sure if they should support the business or support individual employees. And this is where there is a fundamental problem. There should not have to be a choice. HR is there to help the business achieve its objectives through its people. There should be no conflict (unless the business is operating in an unscrupulous way or being wholly unfair as an employer). HR should support the business, help communicate why certain commercial decisions have to be made and help manage any changes that such decisions bring.

The good news is, that when it comes to HR, SMEs can find they have an advantage. Because the responsibility of HR often sits with the owner or director, they can ensure that HR has (and retains) a commercial focus. When putting in the HR foundation, you can ensure it meets the needs of your business and reflects how you want it to operate.

3 steps to the HR foundation

This 3-step plan may not be sexy, but each step is essential:

1. Contracts of employment
2. Human Resources policies & procedures, codes of conduct and standards
3. Implementation and consistency

Step 1 – Contracts of employment

Make sure you have good contracts of employment that give you protection and flexibility. Your contract of employment will either support what you want to do in any situation, or it will restrict you.

When there is an issue or dispute with an employee, the first question is generally, 'What does the contract say?' because it is the contract of employment that will allow you to do certain things or prevent you: for example, if someone gets a parking ticket in a company vehicle, you cannot deduct this from their pay unless you have a clear deductions clause in their contract.

When running a business, you need the flexibility and options that good contracts can provide you with. Good contracts will give you more choices in any situation. Good contracts can save a lot of hassle and are your first step in setting out your rules and standards (we'll talk about this in more detail in Chapter 4).

We will also look at why it is important to have certain clauses in your contracts and some real life examples of how contracts can save you time, money and could even help save your business!

Step 2 – Human Resources policies & procedures, codes of conduct and standards

If the first question is, 'What does the contract say?', the second question will be, 'What does your policy say?'

Along with your contracts, your policies & procedures and codes of conduct will form your rules of the game. How you want things to be done. They will set standards, reinforce what's important to you and define the culture (feeling) of your business. They will help managers manage and set expectations with your employees' and, if enforced fairly and consistently, will built trust and co-operation.

Without these in place, you will be limited in what action you can take in any situation and/or find yourself facing disputes and needless HR issues. We will talk further about these in Chapter 5 and you will see how they can be invaluable in supporting the business.

Step 3 – Implementation and consistency

Implementing and applying your rules consistently is essential. This means you do not sweep things under the carpet. They won't go away... they will fester... and they will end up causing you even greater frustration in the long run.

No one likes conflict (or perceived conflict) and so it can seem easier to 'let things go'. But let them go too often and your rules will not be worth having, and your business will be run by your employees and not you, (and not in a good way!)

Enforcing your rules does not have to be about 'formal disciplinary action' or being an onerous employer: far from it. There are many ways to enforce your rules, and many tactics and strategies you can employ. But the starting point has to be to define and confirm what your rules and standards are and to clearly communicate these.

Putting clear rules in place will also stop many of the 'issues' arising in the first place. The majority of people will play by the rules if they know what they are. And for the minority who don't, having your rules in writing (and clearly communicated) will allow you to deal with any matters more quickly (and amicably).

I appreciate that contracts and policies are only pieces of paper! But they are really important pieces of paper that help you manage your business and ensure you meet some important legal requirements (which we will cover in later chapters). And these pieces of paper will become more than this. Applied consistently, they will reinforce how you do things and how you work, while also providing protection.

Not having clear rules can lead to all sorts of disruption, bad feeling and even disputes. It can waste management time and distract you from taking your business forward. Let me give you an example. The situation described below is a real example of what happened in one SME.

Case study

A company, let's call it Flintstones Ltd., has never had written contracts of employment and doesn't have any policy documents. It prefers to keep things informal and friendly. It is not a bad employer; in fact, the managers pride themselves on being nice and even generous to employees.

Flintstones has a new employee who joins the company, let's call him Barney.

Barney goes off sick for a day and, because the managers want the company to be a 'good' and 'nice' employer, they decide to pay Barney as normal. All is well.

Soon after, Barney goes off sick again for another day and so, wanting to be good and nice, they again pay Barney.

Barney goes off sick for a third time. The managers are now becoming concerned about the level of absence. They also have to be careful of costs and so decide, on this occasion, that they will not pay Barney.

Barney is now upset. From his point of view, he expects to get paid. The company paid him before, so he had assumed that this was the norm and part of his terms of employment. From the company's point of view, they don't have a sick pay scheme and were trying to be 'nice' and generous.

The problem is that this is not written down anywhere, so how was Barney supposed to know? In addition, the employer may have created a contractual right through custom and practice.

If the company had clearly set out that they do not pay company sick pay, the response from Barney would have

35

been different. He would have appreciated the fact that he was paid when off sick the first time and would not be under the assumption that he had a right to be paid each time he was off. The objective the company was trying to achieve i.e. to exercise its discretion and 'be nice' would have been realised – rather than the absolute opposite.

This is just one of many real workplace situations where lack of clarity (and those important documents) can lead to conflict. Rules on sick pay should be included in your basic HR foundation (along with many other things – see Chapter 4).

So, clear and well-communicated rules help you manage your employees' expectations. In the above situation, an expectation to 'be paid' could instead have been seen as 'my employer has been generous and paid me when they didn't have to'. The former leads to disputes, the latter leads to employees feeling valued and building trust.

A quick note: if you do exercise discretion, as in the above scenario, you must exercise it fairly for all employees.

Please let me be clear, talking about contracts of employment and rules is NOT about being an onerous employer. To the contrary, providing clarity for employees and setting boundaries makes for a much fairer (and happier) working environment. People like clarity and boundaries. It gives structure and a sense of security and wellbeing.

Ultimately you can decide what clauses you have in your contracts and what rules you need for your business (maybe with some help along the way and working within employment law), but your rule book does not have to be unfair.

Even if you are a trendy and relaxed employer, with everyone sitting on beanbags, you still need rules – they just need to be appropriate for your business (but talk to your Health & Safety person about working on beanbags!)

On a commercial note, this is about protecting the business, which ultimately will protect everyone in the business. Look after the business and the business can look after its people.

If you don't have time to put in your foundation, then you can get help and it will be a great investment for your business. This is something we help businesses with all the time, and it can be really useful to have someone you can discuss things with and guide you through the legal side. But, make sure that you take ownership and any documents that are drafted reflect your standards and your rules.

Beyond the foundation

We will go into more detail about each element of the foundation in the coming chapters, but what's beyond it?

Well, having your foundation will build consistency, which will build trust. We have all heard the saying 'firm but fair' and most business owners would be happy to be described like this. Your foundation will allow you to be firm, in a way that your employees can see for themselves is fair.

The next steps are to look in more detail at how you can support and develop your people. I'm not trying to be 'pink and fluffy'; this is about a serious commercial approach. Quite simply, the better your people are at doing their job, the more engaged they are and the better your business will be. So, the most commercial thing to do is to help them to be better.

Once you have set out your HR foundation, it will be easier to be clear about the purpose of each job, what needs to be achieved and how success will be measured (your performance indicators). Knowing this will help you recruit the right people for your business in the first place. (I'll expand on this in Chapters 5 and 7)

Once you have the right people in place you need to provide the environment, support and training to help people develop further and continue to succeed. We'll take a look at how you can achieve this, often in ways that do not have to cost a fortune. We'll also discuss how training and development is a joint responsibility i.e. between the individual and the business. So, the first step is contracts of employment, however before we talk about these, I want to address one more critical question which is becoming ever more important with today's rapidly changing work culture – just who are your employees?

Chapter 3 – Employment Status

You need to know who is on your team.

In this short chapter let's look at employment status and why it's important for you to understand this, in order to be in control and manage risk.

Before we talk about the contract of employment and what terms you need and why, it's worth confirming who you need to issue a contract of employment to.

Sounds like a simple and obvious question, and often it is. But not always. I'm talking about 'employment status' i.e. when is someone an employee and when are they not?

This can be a tricky question and has been and continues to be the topic of case law and regulation. The problem is that there are different ways people are engaged and each situation has to be looked at on its own facts.

Employment status can fall into one of the following:

- Employee
- Worker
- Genuinely self-employed. And when it comes to being self-employed, someone may be a sole trader or have their own limited company.

To compound the problem, there are tax issues to consider, with HMRC regulations around 'off-payroll' workers and potential tax liabilities for getting it wrong. For example, those who work through their own limited company but are really doing the same job as an employee, should be taxed at source i.e. in the same way as employees.

This is a changing area, so I am only going to give a brief overview and I recommend that you take advice if you are unsure what employment status someone has or how to engage someone, especially if someone does not want to be an employee. I'm afraid it's not just a case of you agreeing with an individual how they want to be engaged, because the taxman can still come after you and the individual can still try to claim a different employment status, as we shall see below.

So, a quick round up:

In most situations it will be obvious that someone is an employee. You will have a job role that needs to be filled with clear duties, certain hours of work, a salary or hourly rate. You will generally control/manage what the employee does on a day to day basis and they will be required to attend work as agreed. Don't over think this; they are an employee.

You then have someone who works for you on an ad-hoc basis. Now and again. Sometimes they will not be available when you call, but that's ok, they are not obliged to work. These people would generally be classed as workers (or casuals).

You may then have someone who you engage to carry out some specific work. For example, you contract out your PR to a freelance PR consultant who has set up their own business. They will have several clients; they use their own expertise to carry out the work and they control how they do it. They may visit you, but generally they work from their own premises and provide their own equipment. They will invoice you and even risk not being paid. Whether they operate as a sole trader or through their own limited company, they are genuinely self-employed.

So what's the problem?

Well the problem is, it's not always that clear. For example, you employ a self-employed bookkeeper. They work for you, at your premises, two days a week, every week. They use your equipment; they don't have any other clients. You pay them for all the hours they work (so they have no risk). Are they genuinely self-employed or just a part time employee?

What about the self-employed plumber who provides services to a larger plumbing company on a contract/self-employed basis? He wears the larger company's uniform and uses their vehicle (because it's part of the company image). He also has a few other customers as a self-employed plumber. Is he genuinely self-employed or a worker or an employee of the larger company?

And why does it matter?

It matters because of tax and employment rights.

- An employee is taxed at source and will accrue all employment rights.
- A worker will be taxed at source and will accrue some employment rights.
- A genuinely self-employed person will sort out their own tax and has no employment rights.

The advantage to an individual of being self-employed is that they can pay less tax, especially if they claim back their own business expenses. The company who engages them will also pay less tax because they are paying for a flat rate service, in addition to this they will not have to worry about employment rights, as genuinely self-employed people do not accrue 'employment' rights. So there are some clear advantages to engaging people on a self-employed basis. BUT this is not the whole story, because if you get it wrong it can be **very** costly.

We have seen case law where individuals have worked on a self-employed basis and then, when the company says, 'Thank you, we don't need your services anymore,' the individual has then claimed employment status. Where they have been successful, the company has faced claims for unfair dismissal, wrongful dismissal and back pay for holiday.

Where a company employs a limited company contractor, who is just a disguised employee, the business can be liable for non-payment of any tax and National Insurance that would have been due had the individual been engaged correctly (known as IR35).

The truth of the matter is that the government wants to find employment status wherever they can for tax purposes, and many recent decisions at employment tribunals are finding employee or worker status when challenges are made.

What does this mean for you? Well, if in doubt take professional advice, or the safest route is to just accept that someone is an employee in all but the most obvious cases.

That way you are in control and can protect yourself, rather than be faced with potential claims, liability and tax bills – or an expensive legal defence!

And the plumber was...

Above, I asked the question about the self-employed plumber who provides services to a larger plumbing company on a contract/self-employed basis. Is he genuinely self-employed, a worker or an employee of the larger company?

Well, each case will be assessed on its own facts, but in the 'Pimlico Plumbing' case (a real life legal case), the individual was found to be a worker. This meant that he was due holiday pay and accrued other worker rights.

And the bookkeeper...

If she is working at the company premises on regular days, week in, week out, using the company equipment and has no risk regarding being paid, she is probably an employee.

NOTE

For tax purposes there is an HMRC status checker that will give you a good indication. Just look up 'HMRC status checker' on the internet.

For the rest of the book we're just going to focus on employees (those who will have a contract of employment).

If you also have workers in your business, many of the areas we cover will be applicable to them i.e. you will still need workers to follow your rules and work to your standards. They are also entitled to a 'Written Statement of Terms', something I will discuss in Chapter 4. But, as workers, they should not be issued with a contract of employment (as this would make them employees!)

With regard to people who are self-employed, if you are in any doubt about their status I would recommend taking professional advice. The problem is that there are two areas to consider: TAX and employment law. So please take advice from both your accountant and an HR/employment specialist.

Chapter 4 – Contracts of Employment

In football a professional player would never join a new team without having a contract in place.

The contract of employment is an important part of your rulebook and it's far too important to leave it to chance or goodwill down the road!

Before we get into contracts in detail, let's just talk generally about rules around people within a business.

Oddly, although people are a major component in successfully running any business, owners of SMEs often give little dedicated time to planning and establishing the rules around people within their company. Many of the rules often just kind of happen as and when the need arises.

When it comes to employing people, there are different principles you need to be aware of and follow.

External rules and regulations

There are clearly external rules and regulations around HR, with employment law and any industry regulation (more on this later), but provided you do not deny people their employment rights or break the law, it's up to you what rules you have in place.

For example, just because someone has the right to paid holiday, this does not mean they can take holiday whenever they want. You can decide and put controls in place to make sure you have adequate cover etc.

The enterprise's rulebook

There will be rules that you need to set internally in order to support how you want to work and the business goals. These rules are all about setting boundaries and standards.

Apart from some significant areas where the law dictates what you can and cannot enforce, the rest is yours to decide. It's your business, it's your game!

Communicating the rulebook

You will need to communicate the rules effectively so that everybody learns them, understands them and is aware of the consequences of breaking them.

Sometimes either the rules imposed on your business or those you set yourself will change. When that happens, the changes need to be well defined and communicated in a timely manner.

Using the rulebook

And, of course, you will need to make sure rules and standards are enforced (more of this in Chapter 6).

When it comes to managing your human resources, the contract of employment is one of the most important documents you can have (if not the most important). It is the principle means of introducing the rules to people and is the first building block upon which your HR foundation and the employer/employee relationship is built.

A good contract of employment will protect the business and provide it with the flexibility it needs to adapt to changing circumstances, as well as giving clarity to employees. A bad contract, however, will restrict the business, leaving it inflexible to change and vulnerable to disputes (and their associated costs).

Without wanting to turn you into an employment law expert, let's go through this in a bit more detail, as there are some key things that are worth knowing.

Legal requirements include: the timing in which the written contract is actually given to an employee, the specific wording used and the obligations set out for both the employee and employer.

Getting the most from your contracts will take some time and effort, but believe me when I say it will be worth it.

What is a contract of employment?

A contract of employment, like any other contract, has its roots in common law, meaning:

- **It is a promise (or agreement) that the law will enforce.**
- It will exist until it is legally brought to an end by either party.
- If either party is in breach of the contract, then the other party can take legal action against them.

Think about that last point for a moment and what the consequences of legal action might be. If it is an employee who is in breach of the terms of the contract, the employer may be able to justify ending the contract (by dismissing them). Equally, if an employer breaches the terms of the contract, the employee might be able to justify leaving and making a claim against the company.

The law will allow you or your employees to enforce contractual terms, so it is really important that you make sure your contracts of employment meet the needs of your business.

The other thing to understand is that, contrary to popular belief, a contract does NOT have to be in writing. A contract of employment is formed when you offer the job to someone, they accept it and you agree to pay them. That can be (and often is) done verbally. The problem with this is that usually, at this stage, very few of the terms have actually been discussed. You may have talked about hours and pay, holiday arrangements... but probably little else.

Let me be clear on this: if you do **not** have a 'written' contract in place, it does NOT mean you do not have obligations and terms in place with your employees. There is still a contract of employment but, because it is verbal, the terms may be unclear. There is more room for misunderstanding and therefore an increased likelihood of disagreements and disputes!

It also means that you are missing a trick or two as the contract can provide the business with protection and flexibility, but to do so, certain terms will need to be in writing.

TOP TIP

Every time you offer someone a job, make sure it is offered based on the full terms of the contract of employment. Rather than leave it for a later date, send the full contract through with the offer, with a requirement for them to sign and return it before they start or on their first day of work at the very latest!

If you make the offer over the phone, state clearly that the offer is made subject to the terms of the contract (which you will be sending to them).

This way, the potential employee is in a better position to understand the rules they must accept if they are to join your company (or they may choose to negotiate terms).

Your company will also be better protected and in a much stronger position to legally resolve any disputes should they arise in the early days or further down the line.

On top of this it saves on administration – because once it's done, it's done!

What does the law say?

There is a legal requirement to provide employees and workers with a Written Statement of Main Terms of Employment from the first day of employment (as of April 2020, before this an employer had two months to issue the statement).

Technically (sorry to get technical), the written statement is not necessarily the contract. The written statement sets out the minimum information that you legally need to provide to your employees and/or workers.

The requirement to provide written terms (the written statement) from day one, acknowledges the importance of providing clarity to both the employer and employee about the 'rules of the game'. However, the information you are legally obliged to provide is quite basic and does very little to support or protect your business.

So, my best advice is to issue a full contract of employment, ideally before employment starts, but at the latest on the first day of employment. If you include in your contract the requirements of the written statement you will only have to issue one document. If you are a bit of an anorak and want to know where this is covered in legislation it is S1 Employment Rights Act 1996 (as amended).

What should you include in the contract?

Some business owners I come across feel that it is better to have as little in writing as possible. This is normally because they want to change the rules and move the 'goal posts' and don't want to commit to anything. I would, however, advise the complete opposite. The clearer and more comprehensive your contract is, the more protection and flexibility it can afford your company. Generally, more detail equates to less disputes (or to disputes that are more easily and amicably resolved).

But this does mean you need to spend some time to make sure you have the terms you need and consider not just where your business is now, but where it may be in the future. This is where you may want to get some help. We frequently consult on this and play devil's advocate by raising different scenarios and discussing how the contracts of employment will either support the business or not in those situations!

And just to emphasise, when I say clear, I mean that it should be easy to read and understand and not full of legal jargon. The contract is also a communication document.

In terms of what that detail should be, there are two distinct areas to think about:

1. Matters governed by legislation and what is required of a Written Statement of Terms (thus removing the need for a separate document)
2. Matters governed by terms that are important to the company (for commercial reasons and also to support how you work and internal rules)

So, the law (S1 Employment Rights Act 1996) says you need to include the following items in a Written Statement of Terms:

- The names of the employer and employee
- The start date
- The date of continuous employment
- Remuneration (pay)
- When payments are made (e.g. weekly or monthly)
- Hours of work, which specific days and times workers are required to work
- Holiday entitlement

- Sick pay
- Arrangements around pensions (you must provide a pension scheme, automatically enrol employees and workers into it and make minimum contributions)
- Notice period
- Job title
- How long the contract is for (if its fixed term)
- Place of work
- Details of other types of paid leave (e.g. maternity, paternity)
- Duration and conditions of any probationary periods
- Training requirements (mandatory and/or any training the employer will not bear the cost of).
- Any collective agreements affecting the employment
- Terms around any requirement to work outside the UK for more than a month
- In addition, employees must have access to the grievance and disciplinary procedure.

For more details please see the link to Free Resources at the end of the book.

Many of these areas are also governed by legislation that must be adhered to in your contracts. For example, because every employee is entitled to the minimum statutory holiday entitlement, you cannot draft a contract that says you will give less than this. If you do, the law will override it.

Other than the above list, everything else that goes into your contracts of employment is yours to decide.

And even with the items above, you can give clarification and provide greater protection – as long as you do not deny someone their employment rights. That gives you an opportunity to include a range of additional clauses that provide your business with protection and flexibility. Here are some examples:

Conditional terms

Your contract should be clear about any conditions of a new starter's employment. For example, their employment might be subject to satisfactory references, DBS checks, proof of essential qualifications or licences, a successful probationary period, undertaking and passing additional training or a satisfactory medical assessment.

Personal details

A statement around the personal information you'll need to collect from an employee and how that information will be used. This is not just about covering your business in Data Protection terms. Whether or not you can get employees to give some of their personal details might actually have an impact on how your business operates. For instance, if you intend to issue all payslips by email, you might need to stipulate that employees must provide a personal email address.

Company policies & procedures

We'll look at company policies & procedures and standards in much more detail in the next chapter. However, it is important to realise that some of the rules they cover should also be included in your contracts of employment.

Why? Well, the reason comes down to the distinction that exists **between contractual and non-contractual terms.** Where something is contractual it cannot be changed without agreement or going through a process of consultation (remember a contract can be enforced in law, so someone can sue you). If something is non-contractual it can be changed without agreement or the need for consultation (but you should always communicate any changes).

This is why your actual policy documents, standards and codes of conduct should be non-contractual. This gives you the flexibility to change them in line with the needs of the business. For instance, over time, you may wish to change your dress code or your IT policy perhaps.

However, there are some areas that your business will need to be able to rely on legally and some specific clauses/terms that **must therefore be in the contract** to be enforceable. Having them only in a non-contractual policy document will not be enough. If you are silent on the matter, then generally you will be limiting what you can legally do. For example, you would be unable to make deductions from an employee's pay (even for a seemingly legitimate reason such as deliberate damage to company property) without the express written term in the contract of employment.

Case study

An employee of a client had a very bad day... he lost his temper, picked up his laptop and threw it at the wall! There were clearly lots of issues to be resolved around this (e.g. a disciplinary situation arose due to his conduct). But there was also the question of who pays for the broken laptop?
Read on to find out...

Every business is different, but I would suggest, at the very least, covering each of the following points – that all have a very practical application in the workplace (as explained in *italics)*:

- Procedures for authorising and/or allocating holidays. *So you can manage holiday and refuse holidays if you do not have adequate cover – essential for day-to-day operations.*
- Circumstances around sickness (e.g. how and who to report absence to, payment terms, notification and certification). *So you are informed promptly, and in an acceptable manner, when someone will not be attending work and there is clarity about payment – essential for day-to-day operations.*
- Disclosure of information around employees having other jobs. *So you can be sure there is no conflict of interest – or even that they will be awake when they are at work. (A*

client of ours had an employee who had a second job as a DJ... and he wondered why he was falling asleep at his desk during the day!)

- When deductions to pay might be made (e.g. if someone damages property or leaves shortly after going on an expensive training course). *This can be a major source of frustration for employers. You invest money in someone's training and then they leave. Another situation may be where the same employee always seems to damage the company vehicle. Deductions for such situations can be covered with careful drafting (and can deter poor conduct).*

- Payments in lieu of notice. *This can be useful if you don't want someone to work their notice period – and with careful drafting you can also ensure that company property (including a company car or vehicle) is returned on their last day at work... not at the end of what would have been their notice period.*

- Use of company property and its return to the company. *You will be surprised what some people do with company property – from photocopying flyers for the local fete to using their company vehicles as a taxi at the weekend ...yes it has happened!*

- Bonus schemes – especially when a bonus will NOT be paid. *Essential to avoid making payments in certain situations. For instance, if you dismiss someone for gross misconduct I doubt if you would want to pay them a bonus, but a poorly drafted bonus scheme can lead to this happening!*

- A contractual right for the company to introduce short-time working or lay-off (in the event of a downturn). *It may sound dramatic (because it is) but we have clients who would not be in business today if they did not have this clause. It allowed them to reduce their salary bill on a temporary basis to allow for recovery.*

- Restrictive covenants stating what actions might be forbidden by employees for a period after their employment ends (e.g. to prevent ex-employees from soliciting/contacting your clients, or to protect confidentiality or trade secrets). *These can provide deterrents and important protection – but must be drafted carefully to be enforceable.*

TOP TIP

While your contracts of employment should be detailed, they do not have to be onerous, complicated or full of jargon that no one understands. Please avoid this at all costs! Poorly worded or ambiguously worded clauses will be difficult for everyone to understand and legally might prove unenforceable.

Remember that contracts are a communication document as much as anything else, so use plain English, be clear about your meaning and create clear boundaries that people can understand. This is an area where you may want to seek some professional help.

So, my recommendation is to go beyond the legal requirements and establish contracts of employment that cover everything that will ensure you can run your business with confidence. First and foremost, your contracts of employment should protect the business as, in doing so, you are protecting jobs and your employees.

Case study

One client lost a major contract – almost overnight. The company had to quickly reduce its overheads if it was to survive and give itself some time to secure new business.

They had contracts that included clauses on short-time working and lay-off. They took the tough decision to lay-off a large proportion of the workforce. As they secured new work, they brought people back on a three day week, and then eventually back to their normal hours.

This was a really tough time for the business and really tough on employees. It was not a decision that was taken lightly, and the company did the best it could to communicate and explain why it had to take this action.

However, the final outcome was that no one lost their job or was made redundant and the company survived. This, ultimately, was the best outcome for everyone.

The commercial reality of having good contracts of employment is that they can save you time, hassle and money (and in extreme situations can even help save your business)! Let me illustrate some more of the practical considerations we've discussed by means of a more detailed example:

Contractual terms in action

Imagine two competitive companies (Bodge-it Ltd. and Doors for Life Ltd.), both suppliers and fitters of electronic doors. They are of a similar size with approximately six teams of fitters (three people per team), three field sales staff, six warehouse staff and 10 office staff: a total of 37 people.

Here's the difference:

- Bodge-it has never had written contracts of employment and prefers to work on a 'hand-shake'.
- Doors for Life has comprehensive written contracts and they are very particular about making sure their associated documentation is in place (we'll talk policies later).

Now, imagine both companies are facing a number of staff issues and a possible downturn in business around the corner. This is how their options to some of those situations pan out:

Situation - damage to vehicles

Both Bodge-it and Doors for Life have had vehicles damaged in minor accidents and the fitters were at fault.
The vehicle insurance excess in both cases is £500.

Bodge-it outcome (no contract)

Bodge-it have no written contracts and will have to pay the insurance excess and cannot make a deduction from the employee as they do not have the contractual right to do so. Any deduction would be illegal.

Doors for Life outcome (with contract)

Doors for Life have deductions clauses in their contracts covering vehicle excess in these situations. They can therefore make a deduction for this if they choose to.
Doors for Life are able to recoup the £500.

Situation - training courses

Bodge-it and Doors for Life each sent a member of their fitting team on a specialist training course covering new methods of installation. Both of these employees have now resigned.
The course was expensive, costing £1,000 per delegate.

Bodge-it outcome (no contract)

Bodge-it have no written contracts and therefore cannot recoup the cost of training as they do not have the contractual right to do so.
Any deduction will be illegal.

Doors for Life outcome (with contract)

As well as having a training deductions clause in their contract, Doors for Life also made sure the employee signed a training form before he went on the course confirming these deductions if he left the company.

They can recoup the £1,000 by making a deduction from the employee's final payment and/or requiring him to make a repayment.

Situation - resignation in the office

Bodge-it and Doors for Life have both had someone in their office resign, giving a month's notice. They don't really want them to work their notice period and would prefer to release them immediately with minimum cost to the company.

The employee has two weeks holiday they have accrued and not taken.

Bodge-it outcome (no contract)

Bodge-it will have to pay the employee her full notice and should (strictly speaking) also allow her to work her notice as they have no contractual provision to make a payment in lieu of notice.

They will also have to pay any holiday accrued on top of this.

Doors for Life outcome (with contract)

Doors for Life will have to pay the employee her full notice, but they can ask her to take any holiday owing to her during her notice period as this is set out in the contract.

They also have a 'pay in lieu of notice' clause so, after she has had her two weeks holiday, they will pay her remaining notice in-lieu. They will not have to pay holiday on top.

Based on the employee's annual salary of £18,000, this saves Doors for Life £692.

Situation - downturn in work

Both companies are concerned that there could be a temporary downturn in work in the near future. This is due to some planned changes in the industry, and work schedules outlined by a number of larger clients.

Bodge-it outcome (no contract)

For Bodge-it the downturn could put them in a very difficult financial position, which could ultimately place the whole business at risk. They have no contractual options to adjust to short-time working during a downturn in business.

Bodge-it can consider making redundancies. However, there would be a cost to implementing these and, if the downturn is temporary, they will not want to lose their skilled workforce.

Doors for Life outcome (with contract)

Doors for Life have the contractual right to put staff on short-time working or lay them off for a short period. While this would not be a popular decision, or something they would consider lightly, this would be preferable to making permanent redundancies or putting the company at risk.

The Doors for Life payroll bill is approx. £900k per annum (£75k per month). With staff on short-time working for a month (e.g. three days per week), they can reduce their salary bill by £45k. This will help cash flow during the downturn while allowing them to hold onto staff in the long-term.

From these four situations, Doors for Life have just saved £47,192! As well as a lot of time and heartache!

I could go on with the comparisons.

Don't even get me started on the example of the salesperson who leaves Bodge-it to join Doors for Life and starts to contact clients from their previous employer. Without a contract with clear restrictive covenants, Bodge-it can do nothing to prevent this!

Bodge-it and Doors for Life may be fictitious but the situations I've described are real.

Case study: continued

Earlier we talked about an employee who had a bad day... he lost his temper, picked up his laptop and threw it at the wall! And we asked who pays for the broken laptop?

It should be clear from the discussions in this chapter that, without a clear deductions clause in his contract of employment, the company would NOT be able to make a deduction. Despite the conduct issue, it would be an illegal deduction! However, with a clear contractual right to make deductions, the company could legally do so.

With carefully thought-out, well-written contracts of employment, your 'rules of the game' start to become very clear to anyone working with you.

This starts to put your company in the best position to manage HR effectively – giving you options relating to how you want to deal with any given situation and enabling you to legally pursue whatever course of action is best for your business.

The contract also starts to encourage the behaviour you want. A deductions clause that allows you to deduct the insurance excess from an employee if their company vehicle is damaged and needs repair, or to deduct the cost to valet a vehicle if it is not returned in an acceptable condition, will encourage employees to treat company property with respect!

You may feel you shouldn't have to do this, because people should automatically act appropriately, but unfortunately you have to guard against the minority who may not. And it is always the same person who has an 'accident' or damages the company vehicle!

Without a contract that protects you, you can do very little! Are you really ok with **not** having those choices?

(If you are dipping into this book instead of reading it from beginning to end, then make sure you also read Chapter 7 as I'll be explaining job descriptions and why these should NOT be included in contracts of employment.)

Making changes to contracts

I'm often asked whether you can make changes to terms within a contract of employment. As a legally binding agreement, neither party can alter the terms without the agreement of the other. Basically, what that means is **yes, you can make changes but there are processes to follow.**

Most changes can be made by mutual consent. An increase in salary is probably the best example of this. However, problems can arise where one party (normally the employer) wants to make changes that the other does not agree to. When straightforward mutual consent isn't possible, there are a number of legally acceptable options. Here are three:

- You can introduce the *change by agreement*. This generally means going through a process of consultation where you explain the reasons for the proposed change and listen to the individual's views, concerns, ideas and/or queries. Ideally this will lead to an agreement (which may involve some compromises). When doing this, it is important to have a clear process and to document the consultation at every stage. When an agreement is reached, make sure this is confirmed in writing.

- Another option is to create *contracts of employment that already provide for changes* (e.g. with clauses stating possible changes in hours or location of work). While this can make the process of changing terms easier, it is still recommended that you enter into dialogue with the employees concerned and gain their 'buy-in' in order to maintain good relationships. Also, you still need to act reasonably. For example, while it would be acceptable to have a clause that confirmed that an employee may have to work from other locations which may require them to re-locate, it would **not** be reasonable to require them to move to a new location without any notice and expect them to relocate by next Monday!

- If you cannot gain agreement but it remains necessary to make the changes, you can ultimately 'force' the change by ***terminating the employee's current contract (giving notice) and offering a new contract with the new terms.*** (Please do not even consider this unless you have tried to reach an agreement by consultation first – and taken professional advice). The employee then has to decide whether to accept the new contract. The risk is that, if they do not, they will leave and could make a claim for unfair dismissal. An employment tribunal will be looking for evidence that you had fully consulted, considered other options and had a valid commercial reason to make the change.

Clearly, wherever possible, the best option is to gain agreement. In my many years working with SMEs and implementing new contracts, I have never been in a situation where we have had to give formal notice. This is because the consultation and communication process has been clear and everything has been explained.

However, if situations become complicated or negotiations fail, my advice is to keep a close check on whether you are following the correct procedure and seek assistance as required.

Most importantly do not shy away from implementing (or changing) contractual terms that may be 'difficult' if there is a commercial reason and need to do this. Just take advice when you need it.

And ALWAYS document the changes so there is clarity for everyone.

Chapter 5 – Policies, procedures, rules and standards

In football if there were no rules it would soon turn into a game of rugby and it would be chaotic.

If you don't document and communicate your rules, your workplace can become chaotic. You cannot enforce rules you have not communicated. People work better (and feel better) when they know the rules and have boundaries.

Previously I mentioned that when there is a dispute in the workplace the first question is almost always, 'What does the contract say?'.... and the second is, 'What does the policy, procedure or rule say?'

Your company policies & procedures may be non-contractual (I would strongly recommend this - see previous chapter), but they still make up an important part of your rule book and how you want things to be done and will further protect and support your business. So, let's take a closer look at how to use them effectively.

Good policies & procedures provide clarity to employees (and the organisation) about what is expected of them, the standards they should work to, the processes that should be followed and generally how any given situation will be dealt with.

The first thing to say therefore, is that everyone needs to be aware of their obligations. For this reason, you should always include a key clause in your contracts of employment that unequivocally states it is a requirement for employees to follow all company policies, rules and standards that are communicated to them.

But, what policies & procedures should you have?

The key is to make sure you cover areas that are appropriate to your organisation. The policies found in large corporates will not be appropriate for SMEs, and some policies for one SME may not be appropriate for another in a different sector. So remember, when creating your HR policies, to keep things specific to your business. Avoid making them overly bureaucratic, too lengthy or so rigid as to be inflexible, strive for clarity instead.

There will however be a number of 'standard' policies (but written in plain English without being overly bureaucratic) that every SME will need.

Here's why having 'appropriate' policy documents is so important:

- There is a legal requirement to have certain policies & procedures in place (see below).
- Having clear policies (including rules and standards) will help communicate what is expected to employees. The result is you are more likely to get what you want but, if you don't, you can more easily take appropriate action.

- If you have a policy (and procedure) it makes it easier to manage any given situation as you simply follow the procedure.
- Having certain policies in place will provide additional protection to the organisation against wider liability. For example, a policy on anti-bribery and corruption provides a defence for the company in the event that an employee breaks the rules (reducing the company's potential liability).

So, to be legally compliant, your company must have the following policies in place:

A written disciplinary procedure

This should set out the procedure that will be followed in the event of any **formal** disciplinary action being considered against an employee. This is a key policy and we will come back to this in much more detail in Chapter 8.

A written grievance procedure

The grievance procedure is available for employees to raise any concerns they may have relating to the workplace. Many situations can and will be dealt with informally, but the formal procedure that will be followed should be set out clearly.

Equal opportunities

Technically there is no legal requirement (under the Employment Rights Act 1996) to have an equal opportunities policy. However, in my view it is an essential policy. It is the first line of defence for your company (called a 'statutory defence'). More importantly it is essential to make a clear statement that you are an equal opportunities employer *and* to give your employees guidance on what behaviour (conduct and language) is unacceptable and/or may be considered to amount to discrimination.

These three policies are the minimum (and essential) but there are many more HR policies that you should consider. Some of the common ones and the key information they may cover include:

GENERAL POLICIES

New starter information

Information the new employee needs to provide you with when they start and information they need to be provided with *(e.g. probationary periods, right to work in the UK documentation, etc).*

Holiday entitlement and holiday booking

What their entitlement is, how to request holiday, how holiday is authorised and any restriction, etc.

Absence notification, certification and payment

How and when to notify the company if they cannot attend. What payments will be made, what certification they need to provide and when.

Absence management

How absence will be monitored, how unacceptable levels of absence will be managed (short-term, frequent or long-term absence).

Computer/internet use

Your rules on the personal use of company computers, restrictions on websites that can be visited, passwords, use of emails, etc.

Social networking

What can/cannot be discussed on social media about the company, clients and colleagues etc.

Expenses/travel on company business

What can/cannot be claimed, how to make a claim, how people should travel.

Bribery and corruption

What may be considered bribery and corruption, limits on any gifts.

Bad weather

What to do about getting to work in bad weather, what payments will be made.

Whistle blowing

Employees right to 'whistle blow', procedure to follow, reporting internally and externally.

Bullying and harassment

Unacceptable conduct/behaviour and reporting procedure.

Social events

Appropriate conduct for employees at social or corporate events.

Standards

This would include your codes of conduct *(e.g. time keeping, working with colleagues)* and general rules you have *(e.g. around dress code, mobile phones etc.)*

What these all have in common is that they are setting out the company's rules and standards around a particular topic – and therefore if these rules or standards are not met, the company can take appropriate action. Without confirming these rules, the company could not (fairly) take action.

Let's take absence notification as an example. Among other things, your procedure might state the following:

- An employee needs to report absence by a certain time, in a certain way (e.g. by telephone personally and NOT by sending a text message).

- An employee will be required to provide a fit note (medical certificate) after the required period (currently after eight or more calendar days).
- Failure to notify absence will be considered unauthorised absence.

Then, if someone does not follow the rules, you can take action. This may include withholding payment and taking disciplinary action. If unauthorised absence is also detailed as gross misconduct in your disciplinary procedure, and someone fails to notify their absence, you may even end up dismissing someone, especially a habitual offender!

If you hadn't stated your rules about absence notification in a policy/procedure document, you would be unable to take any action! And you would get really frustrated by the situation.

Even though you and I may think it is common sense (and the right thing to do) to let your employer know if you cannot attend work, if you have not written this down and communicated it, your employee may well claim ignorance and come up with the excuse – they didn't know and they weren't told!

Family friendly rights

It is also useful to confirm the family friendly rights that employees are entitled to. Many of these require a clear procedure to be followed. Family friendly policies include maternity, adoption, parental, paternity and emergency leave (and these tend to change frequently).

A very useful family friendly policy is flexible working. The right to request flexible working (e.g. to ask to go from full-time to part-time, change working hours or even request working from home), is now available to all employees, which can sound scary to employers. However, the right is to 'request' flexible working and the legislation sets out clear commercial reasons why a company may decline a request. Yes, there is a procedure to follow but, in my view, it actually makes managing requests from employees for changes in working hours much clearer and easier.

You might also have to address other industry specific issues through policies, as appropriate to your organisation.

Regardless of how many policies you need for the organisation as a whole, there's one important thing to remember. When you do have a policy or procedure in place, **make sure to FOLLOW IT!** There is no point in having a disciplinary procedure written down, for instance, if you are just going to ignore it in practice. That will lead to all kinds of trouble. Your policies are there as living documents. In any given situation, the policy should always be your guide as to how to deal with it. They are there for you and your managers as well as your employees.

When we see claims for unfair dismissal go against the company, in the majority of cases this is not because the actual decision to dismiss was the wrong decision for the company, but rather because the correct procedure was not followed in implementing that decision. This is how important it is to follow your policies & procedures. They are there to help and support the business (not hinder it). They cannot be too vague but should not be overly bureaucratic or complicated. Either way leads to lack of clarity and potential for misunderstandings. It is easy to get it wrong, so seek help when you need to!

Setting standards

Among the suggestions for policies listed above, you'll notice one entitled 'Standards'. It's one I feel worthy of a bit more attention and let me tell you why.

Having a policy around standards (sometimes called 'General Rules' or a 'Code of Conduct') is all about setting out how you want things to be done and people to behave. It's setting boundaries that everyone can understand and appreciate. Communicating your standards will help to ensure this happens from the outset.

Here are some ideas of what you might put into a Standards document:

STANDARDS

Introduction

Start with a short paragraph that sets out why there are standards/rules *(e.g. they are there to help set standards and to support and maintain a pleasant atmosphere for all)*. State clearly that these rules are subject to change (to ensure continued efficiency for the business and wellbeing of employees) and that all changes will be communicated.

Customer care

Do you want to make a statement about your standard of customer care service?

How do you expect your employees to treat customers?

Relationships at work

Do you want people to advise you if they have a 'romantic' relationship with a colleague?

Working with colleagues

Do you want to reinforce that everyone needs to treat each other with respect (and refer them to the equal opportunities and harassment policy)?

Dress code/personal presentation

How do you want people to dress and present themselves? In the office, in front of clients?

Punctuality and time keeping

Do you expect people to be at work and ready to start work at a certain time, or do you operate flexible working arrangements (if so, you need a clear policy on this).

Use of personal mobile phones

What should people do with their mobile phones during working hours? Should they be on, off or on silent? And what about text messages, WhatsApp and other uses?

These are only a few examples of what you might include. For more details (and a template policy on standards) please see the link at the end of the book under Free Resources.

If you find it a struggle to decide on the standards for your organisation, here's a simple 2-step exercise to help.

Step 1 – Write a list of everything that annoys you in the workplace (and consider other areas where you are happy with the behaviours and conduct you see at work - so you can reinforce this). It could be anything from punctuality to the residue of unwashed teacups left in the kitchen at the end of the day.

Step 2 – Use this list to create your standards. It might be something around the expected level of punctuality (e.g. you should be at your desk ready to start work at your start time – *not coming in a minute beforehand and then making a cup of coffee*). Or, it could be a standard that addresses the housekeeping responsibilities for all (e.g. If you make tea/coffee, you should clean and put away any crockery/cutlery you use).

Case study

One client had a 'pet hate' about people hanging their coats on the backs of their chairs. It really irritated him. When I asked why, he explained that he often had visitors and felt that coats on backs of chairs made the office look untidy – not the impression he wanted to create.

Once he had explained this, it was easy to write some standards around the behaviour - and explain why it was important. Most people had no idea that they were 'irritating the boss' by putting their coat on the back of their chair but, once this had been communicated and understood, everyone was happy to comply. With a few words documented as standards, the problem was solved!

Having statements around your standards or a code of conduct within your business will help to set your boundaries and communicate your expectations. With these in place, individuals can then feel free to get on with their job, using their skills and expertise, within those boundaries.

As I said earlier, a lack of boundaries can cause confusion, frustration and stress. People need to know how you expect them to behave.

Tell them about it

I'd like to emphasise a really important element that is often missed. You must **communicate** your rules, policies & procedures etc. to employees – otherwise they are not worth the paper they are written on! I know it sounds obvious, but it is not unusual to find the handbook that contains all your rules sitting on the top of a shelf gathering dust!

'I didn't know! I wasn't told!' is one of the biggest excuses, but if you can demonstrate that you have clearly communicated, you remove this excuse. You will also find that you have less rule breaking, as very often it's not an excuse, very often employees have not been told and do not know!

And you need to continue to communicate, especially when there are any changes. Getting someone to sign that they have seen the handbook on day one may tick a box, but it does little to reinforce the standards.

It is a fundamental requirement of employment law that the employer must be 'fair' and 'reasonable' in their decisions. If someone is not clear about what is required of them or the consequences of non-performance or poor conduct, then decisions could easily be classed as 'unfair' and 'unreasonable'.

If you were told off/disciplined because you failed to report your absence correctly – but you had never been told how to report your absence - would you think that was fair? Or you were told off for making a personal call on your mobile phone during working hours – but were never told this was not acceptable – would you think that was fair?

This is exactly why you need a system in place for documenting the rules, communicating them, managing them and updating them as required. Here are some ideas:

Induction process

Create a new starter list that your company can follow during every induction period. For example, you might want to use this time to ensure each of the key policy documents are read by the employee. You might make a presentation about standards, ask the employee to watch some videos clips or get them to read your policies. You can then have an induction checklist for the employee to complete to confirm everything has been covered.

For a template new starter checklist please see the link at the end of the book under Free Resources.

Employee Handbooks

Many organisations give their staff an Employee Handbook that incorporates all of the required HR policies and standards and provides some general information about the company. This can be a great way to give your workforce easy access to all the relevant information they may need throughout their employment. **But remember to keep the information up to date** and to clearly communicate any changes – as your handbook will change when there are changes in employment law and as the business evolves.

Online

Some companies will put all their policies on the central computer system where employees can access information. This definitely saves time and money on printing, but you need to be clear how these are filed and that information can be found easily. For example, you may put the handbook online (maybe as a pdf document) with a contents page that can link to different policies and information. But again **remember to keep the information up to date** and to clearly communicate any changes or updates.

HR Portal

For a really comprehensive solution, you might consider having your own HR Portal that all employees can access via secure logins. Because we know how our clients struggle to keep these documents up to date, we provide this service via our HR platform YourHR.space. We not only help with the content drafting, but then continually maintain the content and communicate changes to employees. You can find more information at www.yourhr.space.

Whatever method you choose, just make sure to communicate your rules in writing and keep them up to date.

One of the biggest dangers for SMEs is a tendency to put their faith in the **'unwritten rule'**. In the early days, the owner is probably able to control most areas of the business and feels they can easily explain what they are looking for when they personally recruit staff. Quite often, they initially employ people who are known to them (family or friends) and this adds to their feeling of security that everyone understands their expectations. Surely, there's no need to document everything step-by-step?

But this is exactly where things start to go wrong. Especially as you start to grow, as it becomes more difficult to communicate 'how you do things' and to make sure you have covered everything.

For example, the employee who turns up at work on the first hot day of the summer in a pair of shorts – when your (unwritten) dress code does not allow for this, or the employee who gets their internet shopping delivered to the office, when your (unwritten) rule does not allow this.

People like boundaries and they appreciate fairness. If you set out the rules clearly and enforce them fairly, you will build trust. If you then want to change rules or terms it becomes much easier – as your workforce trusts you.

Nothing stays the same

Making (and communicating) changes to your rules

Rules will change.

Firstly, they may change because of changes in regulations/employment law, and one thing that is sure is that employment law is always changing.

Other rules will change because your business will grow and develop, and you will need to do things differently.

There may also be changes that come from shifts in your marketplace/industry; or perhaps there are changing technological or social trends that impact on your company. We could be talking about anything from the social media revolution to the introduction of auto-enrolment for pension schemes.

So, what do you do when you find the rules of your company are outdated?

As I've been saying all along, your company has to remain protected and flexible, so there will be times when you will have to introduce new rules or update existing ones. There is nothing wrong with that – provided that you communicate these new rules to your team and do that in the right way.

For your policies & procedures, things are quite simple. Remember, these are non-contractual (if you draft them that way), meaning that they can be changed as the need arises, without the requirement to formally consult with employees. So, you just need to make sure any changes are well communicated so that your whole organisation follows through with the change and it can be monitored.

As for making changes to contracts, we discussed this in the previous chapter.

Phew!

Over the last two chapters we've covered a lot of ground about rules, standards and boundaries. To summarise, here are the main points to remember:

- Establish the rules for your business and how you want things to be done. There will be rules to ensure legal compliance and those that support your business needs and strategy (and how you want to work).

- Issue contracts of employment that cover the items required of a 'written statement of terms' but also go beyond the legal requirements to protect your business in any given situation. Your contracts are an opportunity to introduce every new starter to the expectations you have of them in supporting the way you want your business to operate.

- Have a set of written HR policies & procedures that make it clear to all employees how matters will be dealt with. Communicate the policy or procedure and make sure to follow it.

- Publish your standards and codes of conduct so that there is clarity about the boundaries you expect people to work within and how they should behave. Don't be fooled into thinking something is common sense - common sense is not that common - put everything in writing!

- There will come a time when you have to introduce a change to your rules. Whether that change relates to a policy or an individual's terms of employment, remember that communication is the key to a successful transition.

A final word

However you decide to draft and implement your rules (e.g. you may get other people in the business involved and/or get help from an external HR provider) you must still 'own' HR and the rules for the business. It is no good getting someone to write your contracts of employment and rule book if you have no idea what is in it! This will defeat the object and there is no way you can enforce rules if you don't know what they are or don't agree with them! Putting in documentation is not just about compliance; it is about supporting the needs of the business. You must take ownership.

Chapter 6 – Enforcing Your Rules

In football everyone is watching the referee to make sure the game is played fairly.

If the referee does not blow the whistle when there is a foul it causes upset and frustration. Worse still, if it keeps happening soon everyone will be fouling. You don't want this to happen in your business.

Just think for a moment what would happen in a game of football if the referee wasn't there. With no one watching over things, wouldn't it be tempting for them to throw that rulebook out and play however they choose? At the end of the day, all eyes are on the final score, so if there's no referee to blow the whistle on rule breaking, why not just do whatever it takes to get that ball in the back of the net?

In business, it's no different. Establishing the rulebook is your way of letting everyone know what type of behaviour you expect throughout your organisation. Everything we've covered so far (contracts, standards, policies & procedures) all combine to make up that rulebook. But, what is the point of any of this if you are not going to monitor things and enforce them?

Whether they are in sport or business, most people want to perform well and do a good job. Most people will also have an innate awareness of 'fair play' and try their best to remain within the rules. However, even while I'm writing this, that old adage 'rules are made to be broken' is ringing in my ears!

So, regardless of how rigorous you think you've been in establishing the rules and standards for your business, at some point they will be broken. Sometimes an employee's conduct will fail to match your standards and/or their performance won't be up to scratch. There will be times when poor conduct or non-performance will be an accident; other times it will be due to a lack of capability. It may even be a very deliberate course of action!

In all cases you need to act – and do so quickly.

Out on the pitch, the referee cannot wait until half-time to pull up the players about their behaviour. There has to be an immediate sanction – a free kick, a yellow card or even a sending off! When it comes to monitoring the rules in your company you have to think along the very same lines.

As soon as a rule is broken, be the referee, blow the whistle and issue the sanction. You cannot wait around for the right moment or ignore it in the hope that it won't happen again. Your employees will be watching what you do just as much as you watch them. If they see you fail to act when someone breaks the rules... well, excuse the cliché, but what's good for the goose is good for the gander, right?

A firm but fair referee is respected by the teams and the fans. An inconsistent, unfair referee is equally criticised.

But here's the problem – most managers working in SMEs just don't like being the referee.

Being the referee means dealing with all kinds of tricky situations involving communication issues, conflict, uncertainty and yes – those dreaded formal procedures. In many cases, this aversion to being the ref goes back to how the business first started, when the owner probably sought out friends and family to work alongside them. How on earth do you issue a reprimand to your big sister or cousin without causing a family feud?

Even if you have not employed those closest to you, SMEs can often feel like a family. That makes being the referee more difficult as you become emotionally involved. This can sometimes be a good reason to have external HR support which can bring objectivity into the situations you may face, reassure you that you are making the right decision and help you implement that decision. But generally, managers will see being the ref as some sort of confrontation and people do not like confrontation.

But, it does not have to be that way and there's a lot more to being the ref than waving the red cards. And, while formal action will at times be necessary, there are lots of strategies you can deploy to reduce the likelihood of things getting that far. When a formal disciplinary does become necessary, there are also measures you can take which will make the process work better for all concerned.

So, throughout the rest of this chapter, we'll be looking at:

- How to nip unwanted behaviour or poor performance in the bud so things don't escalate.

- How to manage a formal disciplinary procedure and implement appropriate action.
- How to deal with claims (e.g. for unfair dismissal).
- The final dilemma – what to do when someone performs well, but whose behaviour and relationships are unacceptable.

Nipping things in the bud!

Most minor problems can be dealt with quite simply by having a clear conversation about them. If you notice someone has occasional timekeeping issues, for instance, then your first step is to have a word with them, ask them why they are not on time and explain the rules and why this is a problem for the business.

To communicate any concerns even further, you can use tools like **File Notes for Improvement**, a standard form that can be completed to confirm when and where improvement is needed. This can also act as a written record on the employee's file.

For example, someone who starts turning up late for work (without an acceptable explanation) could be issued with a File Note for Improvement. It is NOT a part of the formal disciplinary procedure, but rather an **informal** way of confirming what is required (what areas need to be improved upon), which has the added benefit of providing a written record. Some organisations use **letters of concern** as an alternative method, but I prefer the File Note for Improvement as it sounds more positive, and having a standard form that can be completed makes it easier for managers to work with.

If you do issue a File Note for Improvement, it should be accompanied by a conversation with the employee. However, I am well aware that this does not always happen. The problem is that many managers find it difficult to have these conversations and are poor communicators. The best solution to *this* problem is to train and develop your managers. If this is done really well, they will become better leaders and will have less need to have to reprimand anyone. But the reality is, until you can train your managers and achieve utopia, you need tools to help your managers manage and 'force' them to communicate. Even though this may not be the best management style, your managers need rules too, and a simple rule they can understand about having to have a conversation with the employee will help them to adopt the organisational culture you are trying to build.

Let me just remind you here of one of the most important rules you must follow: **the actions you take in the employer/employee relationship must be fair and reasonable.** When it comes to taking the kind of action that aims to improve the performance and/or conduct of an employee (informal or otherwise) it can only be 'fair' and 'reasonable' if it is made very clear to the employee what is expected of them.

In the example above, the employee now has their contract that sets out their start time, access to a standards document that states the rules on timekeeping and punctuality and a File Note for Improvement confirming this. How much clearer can you be?

The good news is that generally employees will react positively to a conversation or something like a File Note for Improvement and correct their behaviour. There will, of course, be some who continue to break the rules regardless, and so you will need to take more formal action, but the other good news is that, if you have already taken the informal measures above, the process will generally be much easier.

Because you have issued a File Note for Improvement (or maybe more than one), you have documented evidence of the problem. This makes the formal process easier, as part of the process will include providing evidence to the employee. You can now provide a copy of the File Note for Improvement (and a copy of the contract and your standards on punctuality and timekeeping) to the employee as part of the formal process.

Finally, as well as being fair and reasonable, you need to be consistent. Even if they make some harsh decisions, a fair and consistent referee will gain the respect of the players and the crowd. A referee who is seen as unfair, inconsistent and biased will be booed and hissed!

TOP TIP

Wherever possible, try to manage conduct or performance informally and don't ignore small issues just because they seem unimportant. Sometimes, resolving the small problem makes all the difference and avoids a much bigger problem occurring at a later date. Nipping issues in the bud can prevent them escalating. Clear communication, informal conversations and File Notes for Improvement can often be more effective and less time-consuming than formal action, while also maintaining good working relationships.

And always be consistent, treating everyone the same.

Case study

A company ran a warehouse operation. Over time the use of bad language became more common and then bad language became the norm day to day. The business owner put this down to the fact that his workforce was unskilled (warehouse operatives) and quite young. So he did nothing about it. Soon, however, he found the language creeping into the office and before he knew it, the language in the office was becoming a problem. He was even concerned about customers phoning in, in case they overheard bad language in the background.

He was still reluctant to act, not really knowing what he could do. Then he received a formal grievance from an employee complaining that they found the environment offensive and felt they were being harassed.

*It was at the point when he received the formal grievance that he took advice. Everything was sorted and he re-established the standards and rules and dealt with the grievance – **but it took a lot of time and money**. It meant taking formal action and following formal procedures. Luckily it was resolved without the employee making a claim to an Employment Tribunal, but this could easily have happened.*

Had he dealt with the bad language at an early stage, and nipped it in the bud, matters would not have escalated. Overall standards of behaviour would not have deteriorated and he would not have received a formal grievance.

No SME needs this sort of distraction and costs. If you enforce your rules and address matters at the time, you are far less likely to find yourself in this sort of situation.

Formal action

It's always best to try and resolve matters informally (through conversations or File Notes for Improvement) and to address matters at an early stage.

However, there will be times and situations where you cannot (and should not) avoid taking formal disciplinary action. This may be where there is a serious matter to address, such as theft, fraud, physical aggression, or where it has not been possible to resolve matters informally i.e. where you have spoken to an employee on a number of occasions or they have received numerous File Notes for Improvement but failed to alter their behaviour.

It is unfortunate but true that, in a minority of cases, some employees just refuse to listen to or follow the rules. There are also situations where employees are unable or incapable of performing to the required standards. For example, the accounts clerk who is bad with figures, or the sales person who cannot close a sale (these will be discussed in more detail in the following chapters). This is normally referred to as capability (or poor performance), but the general disciplinary procedure will remain the same.

I have yet to come across an employer that relishes the idea of taking formal disciplinary action against an employee (whether for conduct or performance). It is time consuming and can be stressful for all concerned. However, brushing the situation under the carpet is not a good option. Formal action can bring about positive results, especially when an employee has previously failed to understand how serious a situation actually is.

Ok, let's get to the nitty gritty of how to handle **a disciplinary procedure** within your company.

The first thing to say is to make sure you get the legal bit covered! Because this is such an important area, I have gone into some detail below but please bear in mind that this will only give you an overview and general principles, and every situation will be different. My advice is, if in doubt, take advice - it could save you a lot of time and money in the long run!

To start with, you should refer to your own disciplinary procedure, which should be in line with the ACAS code of practice. You can visit www.acas.org.uk for further information.

NOTE

One crucial legal point to remember is that an employee has the right to be accompanied at a disciplinary meeting/hearing by a work colleague or trade union official. Even if your company does not recognise a union, the employee still has this right, as they may be a member of a trade union. So don't leave this bit out and include it in the letter you write inviting the employee to the meeting.

In addition to this, you should make sure your disciplinary procedure sets out very clearly what would be considered as **gross misconduct**, usually meaning issues such as theft, fighting or fraud. Think about what behaviour you would consider so serious that you might want to dismiss someone and list that behaviour as potential gross misconduct in your procedure. If you do not include something on the list and then dismiss an employee for it, there could be trouble ahead. Because you have not advised the employee in advance of the possible consequences, a dismissal could be seen as unfair.

If we take an example: a few years ago no one had even thought about the impact of social media and associated sites (e.g. chat rooms) in the workplace. Then, we saw cases coming to the employment tribunals where employees had been dismissed for using social media or visiting chat rooms during working hours or making derogatory comments on social media about colleagues, their boss or the company in general!

Many companies lost their cases and the dismissals were found to be unfair – largely because these companies had no policies on such matters and therefore had not advised employees of the possible consequences of their actions. This is an example of how your policies & procedures need to keep up with the times. (Revisit Chapter 5 for more on this.)

The investigation

When dealing with disciplinary matters, it is imperative that you have all the facts. This is why the very first step in your procedure should be to investigate.

The importance of this stage cannot be overstated, so please never skip over it in eagerness to get the process over and done with.

Investigations should aim to seek out as much information and supporting evidence as possible about the matter that has caused concern. That way there can be less disagreement about the facts. The bottom line is, you cannot make an informed (and fair) decision if you do not have all the facts available.

Here are some examples of the types of information you might need to seek out in different situations:

Investigations
Absence

The employee's absence record is the key piece of evidence in this type of investigation. This should include the reason and duration of each period of absence, and the actual days of absence.

The absence record may demonstrate that there is a pattern to absence (the Friday/Monday syndrome!) or that there could be an underlying medical problem (e.g. if the reason for absences are all the same).

This may help you decide whether to address the matter as a conduct issue (e.g. in a Friday/Monday syndrome you may question if the absence is genuine), or a capability issue (e.g. there is an underlying medical problem).

Conduct

When an employee's conduct is under scrutiny, an investigation must look at the documents that state your rules (Standards, Code of Conduct and any relevant policies) and identify the exact nature of the employee's misconduct.

The information you need will vary but, to give you an idea, here are two examples:

- If an employee is rude to a customer, you should aim to get a statement/letter from the customer and from any other employees who overheard what was said. You will also want to gather information that outlines any enterprise standards relating to customer service.

- If an employee is continually late you would need to keep a clear record of their timekeeping (and the reasons they gave for lateness). Your investigation would also point to the contract that states an employee's start time, your rules on punctuality and timekeeping, and copies of any improvement notices you have issued.

Attitude

Many people think that you cannot do anything about a poor attitude. But you can. A poor attitude can be dealt with, because attitude is about behaviour. Therefore, you need to identify what behaviour is being demonstrated and what impact this is having on the business or other employees.

Attitude is generally about conduct as, effectively the employee chooses whether or not to behave in a particular way. However, attitude problems can then affect performance (as they don't 'care' enough to perform well, even if they are capable of doing so).

In other situations, an employee may be performing well at the job, but their attitude is causing concern in other ways (e.g. they are upsetting other members of the team or are unwilling to co-operate).

Again, your investigation should be about identifying the impact of their behaviour on the business (which includes the impact on their work colleagues). This will probably include gathering examples and getting statements from others.

Performance

Here, the investigation should focus on gathering information and examples about when and how the employee's performance is below standard. It could include task-based errors, failure to communicate information or failure to meet agreed deadlines.

Ideally you will have clear job descriptions and key performance indicators (see Chapter 7) that help to define what is required so you can refer to these during an investigation.

You can then identify the gaps between what is necessary to fulfil the job (from the job descriptions and KPIs) and the employee's current performance.

An investigation can also include holding an investigative meeting with the employee where you can put any allegations to them. This can be a very useful step as this may determine that there is no need to progress to a formal disciplinary (e.g. the employee gives an explanation that 'clears up' the situation) or it may provide important information to help you progress the investigation.

You must document any investigation (e.g. in an investigation report) and, if you do progress to a formal disciplinary meeting, you will need to provide a copy of this and any other information/documents to the employee **beforehand**. You cannot walk into a formal disciplinary meeting and 'surprise' the employee with evidence and documents! That would not be fair. How would you feel if that happened to you?

An example of some of the areas you may consider during an investigation include:

- Taking written witness statements from employees or others (e.g. those who may have witnessed a situation/conduct).
- Summarising who you have spoken to and when.
- Gathering any other written documentation (e.g. letters or emails).
- Collecting any paperwork that is relevant to the matter (e.g. audit trails, records or improvement notices).
- Assembling any additional meeting notes (e.g. your notes from the investigative meeting).
- Gathering other evidence (e.g. CCTV).

TOP TIP

If an employee gives a verbal or written witness statement without you being present, you should always go through their statement with them and document your discussion. This will demonstrate that you have not just taken a written or verbal statement at face value without questioning the individual.

The disciplinary meeting/hearing

The formal meeting is your means of reviewing all the facts and listening to the employee's side. Only then will you be in a position to make a decision about what disciplinary sanction might be appropriate. Therefore, it is really important to do things correctly.

- Allow plenty of time to explain the incident, issues or allegations (and evidence) in full and ask appropriate questions of the employee.
- Provide the employee with ample opportunity to comment on the allegations, put forward their side of events, present any mitigating circumstances and ask any questions they may have.
- Keep a comprehensive and accurate record of the meeting, as the company may seek to rely on this later. You can also consider recording the meeting. Ideally this will be detailed in your procedures but, if not, be open about it at the beginning of the meeting so everyone knows it is being recorded. There should be no reason for people to object as it ensures the most accurate record.
- I would always recommend having two people present from the company in any meeting (especially if the meeting is not being recorded – as one will need to make accurate notes).
- When the meeting is finished, adjourn for a reasonable time to consider a decision. Even when it seems quite

straightforward, you should always review the evidence and what was said before making a decision.

- Confirm the outcome in writing. While it is generally recommended that the employee be told face to face what decision has been reached (with the possible exception of dismissal when an employee is suspended), any disciplinary action must be confirmed in writing.

- Always allow the employee to appeal against the decision and make sure that you detail who and by when they should raise an appeal in the disciplinary outcome letter.

- For future reference, place the meeting notes on the employee's file and provide a copy of these to the employee.

WARNING: Never dismiss an employee on the spot

There is no such thing as 'instant dismissal'.

Dismissal should only ever be considered in cases of gross misconduct or where an employee has previously received a final written warning for continued poor performance or conduct.

In all potential dismissal situations, you must still follow a full and fair procedure **before you make any final decision**. So, even if you catch an employee with their hand in the till, where the natural reaction may be to say, 'You're fired,' don't do it!

Whatever the reason, if you dismiss someone on the spot you will probably lose an unfair dismissal claim (for not following procedure).

If you do, literally, find someone with their 'hand in the till', my best advice would be to suspend them and then follow the procedure.

Just to be clear, there is no such thing as 'instant dismissal'. This phrase is used a lot in 'older' employment documents. What it is actually referring to is 'summary dismissal', that is dismissal without notice. **But you still need to go through the procedure first** to be able to fairly conclude that you will be dismissing without notice (i.e. that you consider it to be gross misconduct, and therefore you are allowed to dismiss without notice).

Remember that the outcome of a disciplinary meeting is not always dismissal. In the majority of cases, in fact, the outcome will be a requirement for the employee to make an improvement (and sometimes within a certain timescale), with written warnings being issued that set out what is required.

So, once the hearing has been held and a decision made, you should ensure you have some means of monitoring the situation.

Right of appeal

The final important element of any disciplinary procedure is the right an employee has to appeal against a formal warning or sanction (including dismissal). Failure to offer an appeal will generally make the disciplinary sanction unfair.

An appeal is an opportunity for an employee to ask the company to reconsider any decision, to present new evidence or provide reasons why they believe the decision should be reconsidered.

Importantly, an appeal should ideally be dealt with by someone who has not been involved in the original disciplinary and who is more senior (or as senior) as the person who took the original decision.

So, on a practical level in your organisation, the business owner or senior director should not be involved in disciplinary meetings, as they should be the point of appeal! However, please note that it is recognised that in micro and smaller businesses it may not be possible to have a different person hear the appeal.

TOP TIP

Any appeal should be entered into with an open mind. It is not just 'part of the process' or a chore to get through, but an essential step in ensuring all decisions are (you guessed it) fair and reasonable.

There may be times when an appeal upholds the original decision and other times when it overturns it. When considering the details of an appeal, if it becomes apparent that the original decision was not sound, be prepared to change it.

Do not be a stubborn referee that refuses to see they have made a wrong decision while the fans 'hiss' and 'boo' at them.... or worse!

Allowing an appeal to overrule the original decision does not undermine the person who took that decision either. It simply makes the independent nature of the appeal clear and demonstrates that the procedure has been followed fairly.

Special circumstances

Before we move on to the challenges you might face in the event of things progressing to a claim against the company, you should be aware that things don't always run smoothly when a disciplinary situation arises.

For instance, it is not uncommon for employees to go off sick when they are invited to attend a disciplinary meeting... or they may raise a grievance against their manager. These situations need to be considered carefully. Should you go ahead with the disciplinary? Should you delay it until the employee returns from sick leave or the grievance has been heard?

The answer will depend on the circumstances of the case and these (as well as general disciplinary situations) are areas where you may want to take professional advice.

While these situations may cause frustration and prolong your procedure, please stick with it. Use the disciplinary procedure to support the actions you need to take as a business in order to address poor conduct or performance. It will be worth it in the long run.

Challenges

You might be forgiven by now for thinking you'll go a little bit crazy if you hear those words 'fair' and 'reasonable' one more time! However, this repetitiveness is one thing I'm making no apologies about - and you will now see why...

When it comes to handling HR within SMEs, surely one of the biggest worries has to be that an employee might make that ultimate challenge to the company – a claim at an employment tribunal.

The most common of such claims are for unfair dismissal and, for once, the law on this is relatively straightforward to understand (but complex in its application!) It states that an employee has the right **not to be unfairly dismissed** by their employer - which means you can dismiss someone **fairly**!

So, if you dismiss someone and they challenge that decision at an employment tribunal, you will basically have to prove that your dismissal was 'fair' by demonstrating:

- That your reasons for dismissal fall within one of the accepted reasons - conduct, capability (performance or ill-health), redundancy, some other substantial reason, or breach of statute.
- That you acted reasonably and fairly in treating it as a reason for dismissal – i.e. that it is gross misconduct or that an employee has received previous warnings (a

written warning and final written warning), but made no improvement.

- That you **followed fair procedures** (and adhered to the ACAS Code of Practice).

IMPORTANT NOTE

There is also a qualifying period for unfair dismissal. This means that currently an employee has to have been employed by you for two years before they have the right to make a claim for unfair dismissal.

BUT there are some important exceptions to this. For instance, if dismissal is related to discrimination (including disability discrimination that may include ill-health or mental health issues), or an employee is asserting a statutory right, then no qualifying period is required.

A tribunal claim will cost you money!

This will include legal fees (although you can defend a claim yourself – but very few employers do because of the complexity of employment law and the time involved), and it is very rare to recoup these costs – even if you win.

There is also the management time involved in preparing and defending a claim - and the distraction from other areas of the business.

If you lose, there would be compensation/awards to the employee as well.

All of this is much more likely to be avoided if you stick to being fair, and the key to achieving that goes right back to having clear rules and good communication – your HR foundation. Everyone should know what is expected of them (and what is not acceptable), as well as the potential consequences of their actions.

Unfortunately, even when you seemingly do everything right, an employee might still choose to make a claim against you!

At the end of the day, you may well win the claim, but it will still have cost your company time and money. This is why some organisations consider pre-claim conciliation via ACAS (i.e. this is where you settle the claim before it progresses) and some business leaders also have further protection in place via an insurance policy that covers employment claims.

There is no perfect solution. The potential of a claim from an employee comes with the territory of employing people. However, a solid HR foundation with good employment practices will help prevent claims from arising, and if you should get a claim, will give you a far better chance of robustly defending the claim. Your HR foundation will reduce risk; prevention is always better than cure.

Chapter 7 – Beyond the Foundation

In football every player knows their position and they know how they contribute to the team. Let's face it, you don't want a goalie running up the pitch to score a goal!

And every player knows how their performance will be measured and the consequences of poor performance. It needs to be the same in business. Everyone has a role to play and a contribution to make and needs to understand what this is and how to do it.

In the previous chapters I talked about the HR foundation and how getting this in place will support your business and allow you to go beyond it.

Having your rules and standards in place (through your contracts of employment, policies & procedures, etc.) is the starting point. You then need to make sure these are clearly communicated and kept up to date. Finally, you need to enforce your rules and make sure people know the consequences of rule breaking.

All this helps set boundaries and provides clarity for your people. People like boundaries and clarity.

But now let's look beyond this foundation to other aspects of HR. As we discuss these areas, it will become clear how the HR foundation continues to support these other initiatives.

Let's start at the beginning – with deciding that you need to recruit someone.

Job descriptions

What have job descriptions got to do with recruitment I hear you ask? Well very simply, you cannot effectively recruit someone unless you know what you want them to do. You need to be clear about:

- What is the job role? What duties need to be performed?
- What is its overall purpose?
- What in the job really counts and adds value?
- How will you know if the job is being done well?

These are not easy questions to answer and the difficulty relates to the complexities of how most organisations actually get their work done. These days, we often have to deal with advancing technologies, integrated work functions, multi-tasking and generally flatter organisational structures. All of this can contribute to confusion and lack of clarity around roles, responsibilities, lines of authority, communication and strategy.

To get the most out of your people and to make sure they are focused on what is important, you need to be clear about what you want and this is where a good job description proves its value. Good job descriptions tell people what you want them to do, to what standard and how they will be measured!

In many cases, you may think it is obvious, but, if you fail to be precise about what you want from your employees (and commit it to writing), then people will most likely fill in the gaps themselves. As a result, they will probably make some wrong assumptions about their position and purpose in the organisation; and even work on the wrong priorities. If you don't tell them what makes a good day, they will decide for themselves. People will naturally get on with the aspects of the job they like the most. Not necessarily the aspects that add the most value!

My boss told me to have a good day...

so I went home.

As well as providing guidance and clarity, a well-defined job description also acts as the starting point in managing an individual's performance. If you are unclear about the job description and employees don't know how they are being measured, how can you then say they are not performing or give praise when it is due?

So, if you currently do not have job descriptions for your employees, start pulling these together now! A good place to start is to ask staff to write down everything they actually do and build up a fuller picture from there. If you already have job descriptions, resist the temptation to jump ahead here, as the key point is to make sure they give people as much clarity as possible. With this in mind, dig them out and review how effective and accurate they are.

But what makes a good job description?

Traditionally job descriptions have been little more than a list of duties that an employee is required to perform. While this helps the employee to know what they should be doing, it does nothing to help them know what standard of work is expected, what their priorities are, how they will be measured or what their ultimate purpose is within the business as a whole and how they contribute. If they see their job as not adding any value or making a contribution they will have 'I might as well not be here' attitude and how focused will they be!?

A stronger approach is to make sure job descriptions are aligned to the business strategy.

JOB DESCRIPTION ESSENTIALS

Consider including the following in your job descriptions:

Introduction

A short paragraph that sets out the overall purpose and objectives of the company and any relevant background information (you can also refer to other documents).

How the job can be performed

You will know how the job will need to be performed. This may include the hours of work, will this include weekends, unsociable hours? Is there a need to travel or to work from different locations?

This may sound obvious, but if you need someone to be flexible with hours, or work unsociable hours, this needs to be clearly identified.

Purpose

Describe the overall purpose of each job role in your business. This often sounds easier than it is.

For example, how would you sum up the overall purpose of a receptionist? Is it to answer the phone, or is it to effectively manage and direct all incoming calls and provide a professional, helpful and customer focused service to all callers and visitors?

Think about each individual job carefully and come up with one or two sentences that succinctly explain what the roles will achieve (rather than what the person does). What is the overall outcome you want to be achieved?

Tasks with standards/key performance indicators (how tasks should be performed)

Of course, you need to include a list of duties and/or areas of responsibility in your job descriptions but it is important to set some standards against each of these. This way, the individual has a clearer understanding of the standards or targets they need to reach, and you have a means of measuring performance against those standards or targets.

As an example, part of a telesales person's job role will be to make outgoing calls. The standard set for this would normally state how many outgoing calls need to be made in a particular time scale. It may be further clarified by confirming how the call should be made (e.g. by following an agreed script).

Good job descriptions provide focus so that an individual knows what their priorities are.

This means they should include (and emphasise) some key performance indicators (KPIs). As the name suggests, these relate to the key areas of the job, the overall outcomes you want to achieve and the performance measures which allow you (and the employee) to easily see if they are on track or not.

KPIs will be different for different positions. There will normally be just a handful and in some cases just one KPI. They may also change depending on the business priorities, but here are a few examples:

- *Sales person – The main KPI will be based on achieving a sales target (but there will be a lot of activity to achieve this, so it could be broken down into the number of calls/appointments made, follow-on meetings – all things which you can use to measure your conversion rate).*
- *Driver – This may include the number of deliveries made. It may also include monitoring miles per gallon achieved as this will reflect their driving style and for large haulage companies could save considerable money on fuel!*
- *Receptionist – KPIs could include answering the phone in three rings (with a professional greeting), transferring calls efficiently, taking accurate messages and passing them on within 15 minutes.*

Consequences (why the standards are important)

You can confirm why you want someone to perform a task in a certain way and to a certain standard and the consequence to the business if this is not done. This helps communicate how important the role is and how they can make a contribution.

Let's take the receptionist as an example again:

- *If the phone isn't answered in three rings, potential clients may hang up and the company could lose business.*
- *If the phone is answered with just, 'Hello,' (rather than the agreed response, e.g. 'Good morning/afternoon, [company name], how may I help you?'), this will give a bad impression, affecting the relationship the caller has with the business, and potentially losing business.*
- *If messages are not passed on accurately and in a timely manner, this may lead to a lost opportunity or a delayed response to an opportunity, or poor customer service.*

Without giving the reasons why you want things to be done in a certain way within your company, your instructions might be met with resistance. The more people understand why something is important, the more likely they are to strive to achieve the right standard. They may even make suggestions how to improve further.

You will know why you want something done in a particular way, but don't expect your employees to know without you telling them. Don't rely on common sense – it's not that common!

Regular tasks

By including any tasks or reports that you want an individual to perform on a regular basis, your job descriptions will double up as a checklist that the employee can make practical use of. This keeps their job description right under their nose and so adds to the clarity around their role.

For an example Job Description (with KPIs) please visit the Free Resources at the end of the book.

Alongside the job description, it is useful to find a way of explaining clearly how the role fits in and contributes to the business as a whole. This will probably be done in a separate document – perhaps by drawing up an organisational chart that shows where the tasks/duties of each employee connect (or cross over) with the tasks/duties of others and the overall function of the business.

In smaller businesses, many job roles will need to be flexible to cover a range of different tasks and roles. For example, it is unlikely you will have a receptionist who does nothing but answer the phone! Your receptionist may also be a general administrator or help out with accounts from time to time. This has to be covered within the job description and so an explanation of how the role fits into the bigger picture is helpful in achieving clarity about where the boundaries lie.

Another useful method may be a checklist of duties with frequency of when things need to be done – alongside measurements and standards.

What if things change?

In a growing and developing business, job descriptions can and do change. Reviewing and managing the changes doesn't have to be difficult, providing you do three things:

1. Make sure to have the right contracts of employment in place (see Chapter 4).
2. Include a statement in the job description that confirms the job role may change and that other duties may need to be performed.
3. Don't make your job descriptions contractual!

In some cases a job role will need to change significantly, so much so that it no longer really exists and a new job has to be created. When this happens, be sure to manage it through a planned restructure or redundancy process (see Chapter 8).

TOP TIP

Review job descriptions on a regular basis to ensure they are still 'fit for purpose'.

- Is the purpose of the role clear?
- Do all the tasks/duties/responsibilities have standards attached to them by which they can be measured?
- Is it clear what priorities should be focused on (through KPIs)?
- Are you using the job description to measure performance?

Only YOU can make a decision about the overall priorities for your business and how the various job roles in your company should work towards them. The benefit of having well-written job descriptions is that they bring clarity about this to everyone else, making it more likely that you will get the performance you want or, when this isn't the case, that you'll be able to identify it and act quickly.

Don't be fooled! Good job descriptions will take time to write and identifying performance indicators may not be easy to begin with. But, to put it simply, if **you** find it hard to document what you want someone to do, you cannot really expect an employee to get it right without guidance. Left to their own devices, employees will fill in the gaps and do what they enjoy most, which may not be what actually needs to be done!

However, once you have good job descriptions and KPIs, this actually helps and allows people to manage themselves and take ownership of their job. For most people this is a real motivator.

Putting in some effort to get your job descriptions right will be worth the investment!

TOP TIP

You can also include a catch-all duty of 'any other duties that may be required to meet the needs of the business' in every job description.

Pick of the bunch – good recruitment

Now we know what job needs to be done, we can start working on how to attract people to our business.

Good recruitment decisions will support your business, while poor ones will weaken it, costing time and money.

If you mis-hire and then have to re-hire, it's easy to see how costly this process can become, in terms of both time and money! But, even this doesn't give you the full breakdown of a bad decision. You may have to factor in a range of other associated costs - lost opportunity, lost productivity, damage to relations with customers or the effect on the rest of your team (to name a few).

Unfortunately there are no guarantees when it comes to recruitment and the only real way to know if someone is right for your organisation (and vice-versa) is for an individual to do the job. However, there are things you can do to reduce the risk of getting things wrong and that is to create an **effective and well-defined recruitment process**. As well as helping you with your selection decisions, having a process in place will protect you against potential liability in the event of someone making a challenge to the outcome of your recruitment decision.

A good recruitment process will almost always involve four key elements, which combine to provide candidates with a clear understanding of the organisation and what would be expected of them:

1. Well-defined roles and a clear person specification (i.e. what skills and experience are needed to perform the role).
2. Appropriate sources used for recruitment.
3. Clear selection processes and criteria for assessment.
4. Offers made alongside the contract of employment.

TOP TIP

In addition to helping you find the right talent for your company, be aware that the recruitment process might be the first experience an individual has of your organisation. It is therefore important that the experience is as positive as possible for all applicants, whether they are eventually recruited into the company or not.

An applicant may also be a potential customer or speak to potential customers. These days, if they've had a bad experience, you should probably also be prepared for a social media backlash!

So let's take a closer look at each of those key elements:

1. Defining the role and the person specification

The first step is to identify that a position exists, defining the purpose, duties and responsibilities of the role and the type of person suitable for the position. We've already looked in some detail at how important the job description is, but don't forget to also think carefully about a person specification. This is what allows you to identify and profile the personal attributes and experience that are required of someone taking on the job (e.g. skills, experience, qualifications, attitude, flexibility etc.)

For example, if you were recruiting someone for your accounts department you would want someone who has attention to detail and is good with figures. Depending on the position, you may need them to have an accounting qualification or be working towards a qualification. You may want them to have specific experience of an accounting package, be computer literate and have experience working in your industry. You may also want someone who can use their initiative and implement required procedures and controls within the accounts function, and someone who has a good work ethic and is keen to progress.

Providing candidates with the job description and person specification at the earliest stage is a way of making what you are looking for as clear as possible. Having these two documents to hand makes it easy for candidates to see if it is worthwhile pursuing an application while also supporting you in the need to be objective when it comes to shortlisting.

For an example person specification please see the free resources at the end of the book.

2. Sources of recruitment

The next big question is: how will you attract the right candidates?

There are many different sources of recruitment you could use, for instance advertising, recruitment agencies, head hunting, online recruitment, job centre, internal vacancies, networking and social media.

To decide what is best for you, you'll need to consider the needs of the business, the nature of the position being filled and your recruitment policy/strategy. Don't forget to keep things flexible so you can adapt your methods for different positions. For instance, you might use a headhunter for a very senior position where specific skills or background are required, but use a combination of local advertising, online job boards and social media for an administrator position.

Whatever method(s) you choose, work from the job description (and person specification).

If you are going to use a recruitment agency be aware that, like any industry, there are good ones and bad ones! To get the most out of the agency you use, make sure they fully understand the position and the type of person you are looking for. You are paying an introductory fee for them to help you find the RIGHT candidate and save you time – not just to send you CVs that vaguely match your criteria in the hope that one will stick! So, give them clear criteria to work to by sending them a copy of the job description and person specification and discussing these with them. Then, ask them to interview candidates for you first. In some cases they may also be able to conduct some preliminary testing on your behalf.

3. The selection process

The selection process you put in place is what will help you to assess and shortlist candidates and eventually help you to select the right person for the job.

So, you need to think carefully about each of the following questions:

- What levels of screening will take place (e.g. CVs, application forms, interviews, group interviews, tests or trial days)?
- What questions will you ask of candidates (in applications or at interview)?
- How will candidates be assessed, scored and shortlisted?
- Who will be involved in the process and who will make the final decision?

The key point in all of this is to make sure that, whatever means of screening you decide to use, you 'score' and 'shortlist' in line with what you have said in the job description and person specification. You do not want to waste time interviewing people who do not have the essential skills, and equally, you do not want to be accused of not putting through candidates who clearly demonstrate all the necessary skills.

For instance, if you have stated it is essential for candidates to have a food hygiene certificate, one of the first means of screening would be to eliminate any candidates that do not have this.

Every stage of selection has its tricky points, some of which are probably beyond the scope of this book. (The question around how to tell a genuine CV from a rogue one, for instance, could probably fill an entire book all by itself!)

TOP TIP

If you do accept CVs, ask every applicant to also complete your own application form – so they have to confirm dates and positions and sign a declaration that this is true! Remember that a CV is a marketing document – and surveys tell us that over a third of people will embellish or lie on their CV!

There is one important element of the selection process that deserves some more attention here – the interview.

When you think about it, the circumstances of most interviews are quite unnatural, with one person (or more) firing lots of questions at a candidate.

Interviewing is a skill that many of us are not well practiced in and so it is not really surprising that many managers find it difficult. In some cases, they are just as nervous as the candidates!

What can you do to make it easier and give you the results you are looking for?

Of course, you can send anyone that has to interview potential employees on all kinds of 'interview skills' training courses or get them to read one of the many textbooks out there. However, I'd like to simplify things, as generally there are only two things you need to get right when interviewing:

Focus on the overall objective

The only reason for interviewing an applicant is to find out as much as possible about them so you can determine their suitability (or otherwise) for the job and be able to objectively and fairly distinguish them from other candidates. The interview should therefore be designed in a way that ensures the applicant does most of the talking, prompted by your questions.

So, while it can be good to give candidates a brief overview of the company by way of introduction, resist the temptation to wax lyrical about yourself or your organisation. The interview is not the time to tell the applicant about you; it is a time to learn about them!

Good questioning

The means of getting applicants to do the majority of the talking is simple: ask the right kind of questions. Wherever possible, use open-ended questions rather than closed questions that allow the interviewee to get away with 'yes', 'no' or another limited answer. Good questions start with openers

129

like 'how', 'why', 'when', 'tell me about', 'explain' and 'describe'. Let me give you an example.

Suppose you want to find out about a candidate's leadership abilities.

- A closed question might be, 'Do you consider yourself to be a good leader?'
- An open-ended question might be, 'Tell me about a time when you have had to lead a team.'

If you ask the first question and your candidate says, 'Yes,' what have you learnt about them? Nothing more than their own opinion of themselves, right?

If you ask the second question, however, you are forcing them to elaborate, giving you a much clearer picture of their ability and experience, and whether that is genuine.

You can take this further by asking follow-up questions. For instance, if a candidate talks about a time when they temporarily stepped up to a manager's position, you might ask them to describe what their biggest challenge was. Or, if they describe a particular course of action they took in a situation, you might ask them what other options they considered and why they chose that strategy.

Remember that all the questions you ask should help you to shortlist your applicants. For this reason, be careful not to ask any discriminatory questions - those relating to a person's gender, race, age, religion etc. For example, it would be discriminatory to choose a candidate based on whether they have or intend to have children in the near future - so don't ask them this question!

Here are some common questions that can be useful to ask (regardless of the position):

COMMON QUESTIONS

Describe the ideal position you are looking for.

This gives you an idea of their values, how they like to be managed etc. If this is at complete odds with how you operate as a business you may have a clash!

What do you know about our company?

This tests whether they have prepared. Have they looked at your website; can they explain what you do? Have they gone further than this to research the company?

What are you very best at? (A variation on 'what are your strengths'.)

This gives people a chance to tell you where they think their strengths lie.

What are you not good at?

This gives you an idea of how well they understand their own weaknesses and how self-aware they are!

Another good one is, 'Tell me about a time you made a mistake, and how did you deal with this.'

131

Tell me about a time when you got x result, and explain how you did it. (The 'x' is something related to the job, e.g. for a sales person, 'Tell me about a time when you exceeded your sales targets.')

This helps you understand how they have directly influenced something – or whether they are more usually just a bystander!

On top of these, you should ask questions that will help you understand if candidates have the attitude you are looking for. It can be tricky to craft questions that are specific to your values but here are some examples:

ATTITUDE/VALUE QUESTIONS

If customer service is important to you:

- What does customer service mean to you?
- How do you demonstrate customer service in your work?
- Give me an example of when you went above and beyond for a customer.

If quality and attention to detail is important to you:

- What does quality in your work mean to you?
- How do ensure your work is of the highest quality?

Draw up a list of questions and use these same questions as the basis for every interview for that position. Yes, you may digress because of how different candidates answer these, as well as your follow up questions, but essentially you will cover the same ground for each candidate so you will be able to 'score' each candidate and make a comparison. This helps make the process more objective.

Getting back to the selection process itself, you might decide to progress from the interview in any number of ways – perhaps by shortlisting for a second interview or using some means of testing.

Testing can be really useful, especially if you create your own tests based on the actual job role. These might be anything from IT exercises, proof reading or typing, to asking candidates to prepare a presentation. A client of ours (which employs telesales people) has an initial role play exercise that gives them some understanding of whether the candidate will be comfortable picking up the phone as well as their basic telephone manner.

In some instances, you may want to consider psychometric/personality testing. This can give you a further insight into the candidate. We are all different and have natural preferences in how we work and these may make us more suited to specific job roles. For example, you might want an outgoing extravert as part of your events team, but a detailed introvert in your accounts department. But remember these are only tools to be used alongside the interview and any other aspects of the selection process. Don't recruit based on the psychometric test alone!

Whatever selection methods you choose, remember that every step should combine to help you (and everyone involved in the process) to make a decision.

When candidates reach the final selection stage, you could ask them to take part in some assessment or trial days in the organisation. Time spent on the job within the organisation can be invaluable for both parties – enabling you and the individual to gain a realistic view of whether the working relationship is likely to be what you both expect and desire (before any offer is made).

We shouldn't forget that recruitment is a two-way process. It is a big decision for any individual to leave one job and join another company. It is a big decision for any SME to take on a new employee. Anything that can help with that decision (for both parties) has to be a good thing. A trial/assessment day(s) will also tell you how interested and committed an individual really is because, if they are currently in a job, they will have to take holiday to come and spend some time with you!

4. Making an offer

As I said previously, it is strongly recommended that all offers are made in writing along with a full contract of employment (making the rules of your game clear from the offset). Whenever a verbal offer is made, make sure it is understood that it is subject to the terms of the written contract.

In addition, I would recommend sending out your Employee Handbook with the offer, and make all offers subject to:

- Satisfactory references
- Satisfactory conduct and performance during a probationary period
- A medical (if appropriate)
- Any other warranties as appropriate (e.g. a sales person confirms they are not in breach of, or subject to, any restrictive covenants when they join you)

So now you have recruited the right person, how do you make sure they are doing the job to the right standard? How do you measure performance?

Key Performance Indicators (KPIs)

How do your people measure up?

So, you've got your rules sorted, gone through your recruitment process and got a bunch of people in place... what more can there be to HR?

Well the next bit is to make sure people are doing the job they need to be doing and to help them do it better. If you have job descriptions this will be the first step – especially if you have detailed what makes good performance.

So, very simply we need to measure how things are going. If you think about any sport these days, they all measure statistics, because this information will help them to perform better. Athletes are not offended by this and don't feel criticised because the purpose is to help them to improve and they are eager to do so. It would be great if this was the same in business.

It's the old adage, you cannot manage what you do not measure (and you cannot improve if you don't know your numbers)!

What I'm talking about is the next step in managing your human resource: monitoring and measuring the performance of your players; keeping people focused on what is important in their role; and taking appropriate action to enhance performance.

So, how do you measure performance and ensure your team concentrate on what is most important?

From the guidance I gave about job descriptions, you know already that performance indicators and key performance indicators (KPIs) can be used to describe the standard by which you want tasks and duties to be performed. They give clarity to the business and to individual positions, telling you and your team what is important – what makes a 'good day'. They are your key to measuring performance!

When it comes to keeping people focused on their priorities throughout their entire employment, one answer is to firstly make them aware of their KPIs and then get them to regularly report on them (e.g. weekly).

Take an accounts person, for example. One of their duties is to manage credit control effectively and their KPI attached to this task could be to collect all money owed within 30 days. Now, suppose they also have to report on this weekly. With this in mind, do you think they would waste a lot of time on some other task (which they prefer to do) or would the requirement to provide a report keep them focused more on addressing the company's debtors?

This same principle can be used for every job at every level. The secret is to identify, for each individual, what information would give you a real snapshot of how things are going and how often you want to see that information. You then need to pass ownership to the individual, for example by allocating them a task of preparing a weekly report. This means the individual knows what they have to do, how they have to do it and when they have to report on it. It also means they know clearly where the buck stops – that if they fail to achieve their KPIs, they'll have to explain why!

One thing to note is that reports don't have to be lengthy or go into the minutia of what someone has been doing.

Our accounts person, for example, will have to carry out a lot of activity in order to achieve their KPI around the 30-day payment terms for the company. They may have to call debtors a certain number of times and issue a number of repeat invoices before getting the actual money. In a report, however, all you need to know initially is the numbers around how many debtors are meeting those payment terms (and those that are not). If the KPI isn't being achieved, you will then want to ask more questions: how many calls they are making, what is the quality of those calls, how promptly are invoices issued, etc.

If you are being kept informed by KPI driven reports on a regular basis, you will find you'll know sooner rather than later where the problem areas are. That puts you in a better position to investigate and do something about it.

While this won't be true of every individual, I believe that when people are clear about what their priorities are, they are more likely to understand how that fits in with the bigger picture and be proud of their part in it. They are also more likely to come up with their own ideas or suggestions for how things could be done better. Our accounts person, for example, may recommend changing payment terms and procedures. For example, they may recommend introducing direct debit payments and demonstrate how this would reduce debtors, improve cash flow, save time and allow them to do other things. This could have a really positive impact on the business.

TOP TIP

Publishing KPIs across your organisation can be a great way of motivating everyone to achieve them and creating some healthy competition.

If you publish KPIs by department, this can also improve everyone's understanding of what different departments do, what their priorities are and how each function of the business impacts on each other.

With greater understanding comes improvement in communication, co-operation and overall productivity.

The last thing to say about KPIs is that, like your rules and job descriptions, you might find you need to change them. As your company evolves, make sure the KPIs you've set are still relevant and that they are not maintaining a focus on something that is actually no longer a priority for the business.

So, look at the information you are asking people to report on and regularly ask yourself why you need or want it.

What is its value and what is it telling you?

If you find it is no longer of any use, don't be afraid to go back to the drawing board. Make a fresh assessment of what really counts in each of your job roles (what takes your business further towards the goal) then make that the Key Performance Indicator.

Your people sorted!

Ok, if you've been following (and implementing) everything I've covered so far in this book, here's how things stand:

- You'll have a solid HR foundation (contracts, rules, standards).
- The positions in your organisation will be well-defined.
- You'll have carefully selected the people filling those roles.
- Everyone will know (and stay focused on) what their priorities are.
- People will regularly report to you on their KPIs.
- Performance will be easier to measure.
- Any failures to meet priorities can be quickly investigated and corrected.
- And, while all this is going on, you'll have the freedom to get on with other areas of running, managing and developing your business.

Chapter 8 – Time to Move On

In football there is a transfer window and it's ok for people to move on. Sometimes because they want to, sometimes it's the manager's decision.

Just because a player does not do well with one team, does not mean they cannot thrive in another. It's the same in business. Someone may excel in a different company and/or a different role.

In today's employment market, a 'job for life' has become practically extinct.

In fact, it is far more common now to see people switching roles and companies with a frequency that just a generation or two ago would have been unheard of.

There's no getting out of it. If you are running a business in the 21st century, an essential part of your HR is to manage and deal effectively with staff turnover. Get this right and the coming and going of people might be a good thing for your business; get it wrong and there could be chaos.

In previous chapters, we've covered much of what needs to be done to successfully integrate new people coming into your business. That starts with the recruitment process and well-written job descriptions and is followed through with new starter processes that enable employees to understand the rules and values of the company. During employment, the integration continues to be monitored through tools such as performance indicators, the result of which is a workforce that is clear about their respective roles and positions within the organisation.

What I'll concentrate on now is what to do in situations where someone exits your company. The reasons why people may leave are numerous.

Some people will leave of their own accord (e.g. resigning their position).

Sometimes a change is necessary for the survival of the business (e.g. redundancies or restructuring strategies).

On other occasions, the exit of an employee may be the outcome of a disciplinary/capability process, or it may be driven by the business in other ways.

So, how can you manage all these different situations (especially the last two) in a way that works best for everyone involved?

When it comes to handling exits in your business, you need to consider the following:

- Practical issues. These include things like notice periods, pay in lieu of notice, restrictive covenants, company property, etc. These will be covered in your HR foundation.
- Following procedures. Gone are the days when an employer could tell someone to pack up their stuff and go. To exit a member of staff, you need to have in place (and follow) procedures! Some, like the disciplinary procedure, will be covered in your HR foundation. Others we will discuss below.

- Communication. Believe it or not, it is OK to talk to people about exits as long as such communication is conducted fairly and that the reason for the discussion is both clear and based on facts (more on this later).

When you deal with any type of exit from your organisation, pay attention to these three points and the exit should be a smooth one.

Practical considerations

When it comes to the end of employment, there are many practical issues to cover. The important thing is to make sure you don't wait until the end of employment before you consider these!

What happens at 'The End' should, in fact, be included in your HR foundation and included in your contracts (and policies) from the beginning.

Some of the matters you might want to cover are:

- Notice period
- Pay in lieu of notice (PILON) and/or garden leave
- Holiday pay/allocating holiday
- Deductions on final salary
- The return of company property
- Restrictive covenants

If you have these areas covered in your contracts, when someone leaves you can then follow your rules in the actions you take. For example, when calculating final salary, you might make a deduction for the cost of a training course (if this is part of your rules and it was agreed and documented at the time the training took place).

You also need to 'exit' a leaver from all sorts of areas of your business. You will need to remove them from your computer system, from any door entry system, you may need to change passwords.

To make things easy, you might want to use the rules you have around termination of employment to create a leaver's checklist to record what needs to be done including the above, from the return of company property to issuing a P45.

A leaver's checklist can be kept on file to help with any queries that may arise post-termination or to respond to reference requests.

As part of your exit process, you may also find it beneficial to conduct a leaver's interview or issue a leaver's questionnaire. This will help you to better understand the reasons for the departure and can be especially useful if the company suffers from high staff turnover.

The practicalities of ending employment will be different from one company to the next but, as long as you make the actions you wish to take clear from the start, your organisation will benefit from the flexibility, control and protection it needs.

For some template forms around leavers, visit the free resources at the end of the book.

OK, with the practicalities taken care of, let's now look in more detail at the different situations that can arise.

I'll start by looking at those times when the exit of an employee is a management decision – these are generally dismissals by the company, but there are different ways to manage these (depending on the circumstances). I'll also briefly mention redundancies and restructuring.

Finally, we'll talk briefly about the type of exits which are (in most cases) made because of the employee's decision i.e. resignation (or retirement).

Exit strategies

Dismissals

Dismissing an employee is probably one of the most difficult things to do, mainly because of all the associated issues that come with it. Operationally you'll have to think about replacing the person being dismissed, training someone new and how you will manage with reduced resources in the interim. There could also be conflict or legal challenges to deal with (e.g. a claim for unfair dismissal). In addition, the whole situation can be emotionally draining, and it is just not a 'nice' thing to have to do!

The 'pain' of exiting someone can result in managers trying to ignore the situation, as it seems easier NOT to address issues! But beware... it seldom is.

In his book 'Good to Great', Jim Collins talks about the situation where we have the wrong person on the bus, and even though we know this, we delay making a decision. We give people endless chances, hoping things will get better. We spend more time trying to manage this one person than the rest of the team, and even put systems in place to help compensate for their failings.

We then take these problems home and our energy is diverted by thinking about them (rather than either relaxing or thinking about more constructive things in the business).

Collins concludes that keeping the wrong people is ultimately unfair for all these reasons and it's unfair on the rest of the people in the business because others have to compensate for their inadequacies.

Sound familiar?

It's a bit like the 80/20 rule. You spend 80% of your time trying to manage 20% of the people. This takes time away from the 80% who are performing well. It can be extremely draining!

So how do you exit the wrong people? And, how can you do this whilst also protecting the business against potential claims?

First of all, some exits are easier than others!

Sometimes, especially in the early stages of employment, exiting the wrong employee can be (legally) quite straightforward.

If you recall in Chapter 6, we discussed how an employee currently needs two years of continuous employment before they can make a claim for unfair dismissal. Generally, this means that provided you end the contract by giving notice, you do not have to go through lengthy procedures and there is no risk to the company. (Please check this at the time of reading as the qualifying period may have changed and there are also important exceptions to watch out for!)

This is another very good reason to have performance measurement practices in place during the early stages of employment. You should know well before the end of the first two years if someone is right for the business. In fact, you should have a very good idea within the probationary period... and sometimes you'll even know within the first week!

NOTE

Many HR people will object to the idea of not following the disciplinary procedures in the early stages of employment - even when there **is no 'legal' requirement to do so.**

My view is that it can be 'kinder' to deal with the situation decisively. Sometimes, it is very clear that an individual is wrong for your business. Is it really fair to go through processes and procedures and put the employee through a whole lot of stress when you know it is just not going to work out?

It can also be the case that someone is right for the business for a considerable period of time (or that no one has actually paid any attention or been prepared to address lack of performance) but suddenly things change.

It may be that the business changes so that it is no longer able to 'carry' a poor performer or that it must demand more from its people. If you have a Sunday league team who suddenly want to go up to the Premiership, many players will struggle considerably. They will not want the added commitment or training regime that will be required. And, most will not have the skill to take you to the Premiership. This leaves you in a position where you have to exit existing players and bring in new ones.

It won't always be easy!

There are many reasons why the needs of your business might require you to dismiss an employee. The most common examples include:

- Issues that are defined (legally) as falling under capability. Basically, this means someone is not capable of doing their job due to performance or illness (the latter is often managed under policies around long-term absence).
- Issues that are defined (legally) as falling under conduct. This is about rule breaking and could include everything from poor timekeeping to theft!

When issues such as these adversely impact on the business and informal performance improvement measures have failed to produce any change, following a formal disciplinary/capability procedure may be the only option. (See more in Chapter 6.)

That said, there are times when I've come across clients who wish to exit an employee, but the reason why is not entirely clear-cut – usually something to do with the employee's 'attitude'. Perhaps they are 'capable' but don't apply themselves. Perhaps they do a good job, but everyone avoids them because they are difficult to get on with. Or maybe the employee used to do a good job but is now struggling and doesn't seem as engaged – displaying a negative attitude!

From the business owner's perspective, a member of staff who has this kind of poor attitude can be one of the most destructive and difficult to work with. If someone is negative, making silly mistakes and undermining others (including management), it can be very tiring! The problem is the 'bad attitude' can often be very subtle – a comment here or there – but just not quite enough to pin down.

A clash of values can lead to similar concerns. What do you do about the aggressive salesperson who gets results but leaves a bad reputation in his/her wake? Or, how about the receptionist who is efficient but on the verge of being rude to callers?

You might find that attitude problems are a reaction to a particular management style. For example, if an employee has been 'allowed' to get away with certain behaviour, they will probably continue with it. Sometimes it is a reaction to change. If your business is growing, the employee who joined the company when it was smaller might start to feel marginalised and consequently feel less involved, less valued and so less engaged.

'Attitude' issues are all about behaviour and values - how someone chooses to conduct themselves or thinks it is acceptable to act! Just one individual's bad attitude can make a big impact on your business and other members of staff, but dealing with it (and possibly taking it to the point of dismissal) seems fraught with danger. Scared off by the fear of a legal complication or a natural aversion to confrontation, many managers will 'put up' with a bad attitude rather than face or deal with the problem.

Be warned: this is a big mistake!

Difficult situations have to be faced. Leave things like poor attitude to go unchecked for too long and the frustrations (and the impact on the business) will just grow and grow.

I recall a new client who had an individual like this, and when I asked how long it had been going on, they said, 'Years!'

Years where no one in management had been prepared to address the situation (because of fear of confrontation, litigation and a belief that they could not do anything about it). And, with no one challenging the behaviour, it continued. People walked on eggshells around this employee and at least two people had left the company because this individual was so difficult to work with.

When the matter was finally addressed – and it did take some time because it had been allowed to go on for so long – there was a noticeable change in the whole atmosphere and there were much happier and more positive employees. This in turn had a positive impact on productivity and customer service (and staff turnover).

What is interesting is that generally if one party is unhappy, so is the other! If you are stressed out because of someone's lack of performance, poor attitude or general conduct, you'll probably find that they are too.

An exit strategy will give an opportunity for this to be addressed.

Sometimes an exit strategy will help people to make a decision they want to make but are frightened of. They don't want to continue working in your company, but are worried about the implications of leaving, not least the financial consequences.

We had a situation with a client who had an employee who was just not suited to the job she was doing. She did not have a poor attitude – in fact she was very popular, but she continually struggled in the role. The client even became concerned that she would make herself ill if she continued. It just so happened that the client had a business associate who ran a very different business and they had the perfect position for the employee. This is the sort of exit strategy that is good for everyone.

The simple answer is to start a dialogue

If you are trying to help someone move on, it is in your and their best interest that this is done quickly and as amicably as possible. To achieve this, the best tool you have is dialogue...

communication... a proper chat. Whatever you prefer to call it, talking openly about the issues is your best chance of a quick resolution.

TOP TIP

You may think that you cannot speak to an employee about an exit as this could lead to a claim for constructive dismissal.

Generally, you would be right, as constructive dismissal is when the company acts or behaves in a way to seriously breach the contract of employment. This can include acting in a way to make the employee resign (you can see how this situation could arise if you sit down to talk about an exit!)

Constructive dismissal can be any serious breach of contract, for example, not paying an employee or demoting them for no reason, forcing an employee to accept unreasonable changes to conditions of employment without agreement (see Chapter 4 and contracts of employment), bullying, harassment or violence against employees.

However, you can talk to employees about your concerns – how they are performing, or how they are acting or conducting themselves, or even that you are concerned for their wellbeing and why.

You can also have a 'protected' conversation about a settlement agreement. The legislation around this allows you to discuss an exit strategy – but protects you from the employee then using this to make a claim for constructive dismissal at an employment tribunal (see Settlement

Agreements later). You should always take professional advice on this before entering into a protected discussion/settlement agreement.

Whether you make it a formal or informal conversation is up to you and will depend on the nature of the behaviour, relationship between the employee and manager, and what level of clarity is required in any given situation.

In some cases, an informal conversation explaining your concerns about their performance or conduct may be enough for the employee to change their behaviour or performance ('buck up their ideas') and so negate the need to take things any further. In other cases, a more formal process may be appropriate so that it is very clear to the individual where the problems lie.

The key point is that you must be honest with your employees because 'carrying' someone who is not performing will be bad for the business, for them, and other employees.

In his book 'Winning', Jack Welch talks about differentiations. This is a system that provides clear performance management so that people are very clear about where they stand in the organisation (and that they may be exited if they are not performing). In answer to his critics about this process, Welch talks about how unfair it is NOT to be honest with people about how they are performing.

He talks about how we continue to employ people who are not performing because they are nice individuals. But the fact is that protecting under-performers always backfires. People *will* know if someone is under-performing and, if it's not dealt with, it will cause resentment.

But most importantly it is not fair on the individual who is under-performing. How can they possibly improve or develop if they are oblivious to the fact that they are under-performing? This does not put them in a good position within the business, as they will never progress (unless they are promoted out of a position to move them on ...and yes this does happen). These people are often the first to be made redundant when there is a downturn and have no idea why.

So, as part of your HR, you may well have to deal with some individuals who are in denial and unwilling to accept that there is a problem (especially if it has been allowed to go on for some time) – or they may expect the company to just 'put up' with how they are until they 'sort themselves out', in which case a formal disciplinary procedure must be followed. Other times, a conversation might highlight some problem that the manager was unaware of (perhaps an issue outside of work), in which case you can be supportive while careful to ensure any long-term detrimental impact on the business is avoided or dealt with appropriately.

Opening up a dialogue about your concerns could lead to many outcomes. It may include offering the employee a new role that suits them better, or discussing an exit and agreeing a settlement arrangement that allows them to move on to expand their experience or do something completely new.

Case study

With one client, who ran a car dealership, they had a conversation with an employee in sales who was seriously underperforming. They asked why and what could be done. The outcome of the meeting was that the employee really did not like the role he was in. He loved cars, but really wanted to be a mechanic. They agreed to train him and he has turned out to be one of their most positive, productive and loyal employees.

Settlement agreements

The law recognises that sometimes things just won't work out and therefore allows for a termination of employment via a settlement agreement.

In simple terms, this allows both parties to enter into dialogue about an exit (if both are agreeable to do so and they follow certain rules) and **agree** the terms under which an employee will leave the company.

It is a legally binding agreement (which can be proposed by either the employer or employee) and, once agreed, it will prevent a claim being made against the company for unfair dismissal or other claims (provided it is actioned and drafted correctly). Generally, a payment to the employee concerned will be negotiated as part of the agreement.

So, when would you use a settlement agreement?

Well, let's suppose there is an issue with an employee's performance or conduct and a disciplinary procedure is either about to be instigated or has already begun. As we know, such lengthy and time consuming procedures can be difficult and stressful for both the employer and employee. This is where a settlement agreement could be an attractive option.

An employee might well suggest a settlement agreement as they would prefer this to the prospect of having a formal warning on their file or being dismissed.

However, it is more common for the employer to propose a settlement agreement, the benefits being that it can avoid the need for disciplinary action, save management time and ultimately bring the employment of the 'problematic' employee to a much quicker (and possibly more amicable) end.

Most importantly, **if an employee accepts a settlement agreement, they will be signing away their right to make a claim for unfair dismissal (and other claims).** This provides the company with certainty about the outcome of the situation. However, as always, you must do things properly and stick to the rules. The key points to be aware of are:

Settlement agreements are voluntary – Neither party is obliged to accept the agreement or even enter into a discussion about them. If you speak to an employee about a settlement agreement but act inappropriately (e.g. you discriminate or attempt to force a conversation when the employee has stated they do not want to discuss a settlement) you may find that they can rely on the conversation later and this could be grounds for constructive dismissal.

To be legally binding, there are formal conditions which must be met – These include making sure that the agreement is in writing and the employee **MUST take independent legal advice** from a solicitor or a certified and authorised member of a trade union (and in most cases, the company will pay for this advice).

Be clear about the wording – As with any legal document, it is advisable to take professional advice on this, as the specific wording of any agreement can be important to ensure the company is fully protected and that all matters have been considered.

Case study

In one agreement, a company agreed to allow the employee to keep their company car for three months following the date of termination.

What they failed to say was that, in the event that the employee secured alternative employment, they were not permitted to use the car to carry out work for another company or for other commercial reasons.

When the employee landed a job as a field salesperson and started using the car, the company was less than pleased.

So careful drafting is important.

So, what happens at the end of it all?

If an agreement is reached, any disciplinary procedure that is underway will come to a stop, the practicalities of ending the employment will begin and any payments agreed will be made.

At this stage, remember the employee has waived their right to make a claim at an employment tribunal about any issue that is listed on the agreement. However, you should be aware that there are circumstances when a claim could still be made, for instance if you failed to adhere to the formalities (including those mentioned above) or if you do not comply with the terms of the agreement!

Why make a payment to an employee for not performing?

Many clients have asked, 'Why would I pay someone anything when they have not been performing/conducting themselves appropriately?'

Looking at any situation objectively and commercially, it is about comparing the cost of making a payment to an employee with the cost of keeping them in the business. Think about the impact in terms of lack of performance, lost opportunity, impact on the rest of the team, the stress it causes you and the time involved in going through the right procedures.

If it will take you three to six months (or more) to go through a performance management process, maybe it is easier and in the best interest of both parties to at least discuss a settlement agreement?

And ask yourself if the situation could have been managed better at an earlier stage? Have you or your management team managed the employee appropriately during their employment? If you have failed to address poor performance or conduct at an early stage (and now it has escalated or you have become completely frustrated by the situation), then you need to take some responsibility.

Even in cases of misconduct, you may want to consider a settlement to prevent the need to go through lengthy investigations and disciplinary procedures (but with the added certainty that the employee will have to leave and will not be able to make a claim).

Every situation will be different – and settlement agreements are just one of the practical tools to be aware of. They shouldn't, however, be considered as a standard substitute for dealing with any 'issues' or to replace formal disciplinary/capability procedures (and you do not want to get a reputation for 'paying people off' as this can send the wrong message). There will be times when a settlement agreement is appropriate and times when it is not.

Before you hold any discussions with an employee, it is wise to seek professional advice.

Some other substantial reason

Our discussion would not be complete without looking at other situations that may arise that do not fall within the definition of conduct or performance, but entail 'some other substantial reason' why you may need to consider exiting an employee.

You may remember that this particular phrase was listed among the 'fair' reasons for dismissal when we talked about being the referee.

Some other substantial (SOS) reason is really a catch all term for circumstances that do not fall neatly under conduct, performance or redundancy (see below), but which might still result in a business identifying a need to consider taking action or dismissing someone. Most SOS reasons relate to where there is a commercial 'risk' to the business and demonstrate how employment law recognises that businesses need to operate within the commercial world. However, these can be really difficult situations to deal with because, as you will see from the examples below, often the employee may have done nothing wrong!

A couple of examples (taken from real cases) may explain this better:

Case study 1

Take a situation where you have a husband and wife employed by the same company. He is their top salesman but resigns to work for a competitor.

The company is, understandably, concerned that the wife may pass on information to her husband that could be damaging to them. In a small business it may be very difficult, if not impossible, to keep sensitive information away from the wife. This may include potential prospects, product information, marketing strategies and pricing.

The bottom line is, that even though she has done nothing wrong, the company may have to consider taking action, which could entail anything from changing her job role (so she does not have access to sensitive information, hence removing the risk) to dismissing her.

Even if it were possible to move her to another position, the company would need to justify this decision as she may object and claim constructive dismissal. If there is no way of removing the risk, ultimately the company may have to dismiss her.

Case study 2

Another example might be where a client puts pressure on a company to remove an employee from their site (e.g. a security officer at a client's premises).

In these cases, you should ask the client to reconsider and the business will also need to look at redeployment (if this is possible). However, if it turns out that your contract with your client is at risk, and there are no other options available, you may have to dismiss the employee.

In such situations... yes, you have guessed it... there is a procedure to follow that includes investigating the situation, looking at all other options first and making sure you take into account what the employee has to say (so, while it may not be called a disciplinary procedure, a similar procedure would be followed).

Redundancy

A redundancy situation can occur if the business itself comes to an end but, most often, it arises when the needs of the business have changed so that a certain type of work is no longer required or that work has reduced so much that a particular job function is no longer viable.

What you must remember is that a redundancy **is a dismissal**. Like any other dismissal, redundancies must be made 'fairly' and there are rules to follow. This means:

- It must be a genuine redundancy and fall within the legal definition (as above).
- Fair selection criteria must be applied to identify which employees may be made redundant.
- The company must consult with employees about the situation.
- The company must consider alternatives to redundancy.
- Redundancy payments must be made to employees in accordance with statutory redundancy, their contract of employment or any enhanced redundancy policy held by the company.

I should just point out that if you are making more than 20 redundancies, there are additional procedures to consider, including collective consultation and minimum periods of consultation.

So, please take this as an overview of how to prepare for possible redundancies. My purpose here (as with this entire book) is to demonstrate that, as a business owner, you have options about how you run your business (provided you operate within the law and follow the right procedures). You need to be making decisions that are right for your business. Taking the decision to make redundancies may be tough but, very often, if you do NOT act, the entire business (and all jobs) can be at risk. No one said it was easy running a business.

Employment law will support you - provided you have the commercial need/requirement to make the changes and you follow the right procedures, make appropriate payments and act fairly.

Here are some of the key areas to consider:

A fair selection

The first thing an employer has to do is to identify who is at risk of redundancy and justify why they have been selected.

Where the same (or similar) job function is carried out by a number of people, this means initially identifying the 'pool' of staff at risk. For example, if you need to reduce the number of operatives in a warehouse, you should put all your warehouse operatives into the 'pool'. Failure to identify the appropriate pool could make the redundancy unfair.

The next step is to score all the employees within the 'pool' using selection criteria that offer as much objectivity as possible (e.g. skills, experience, qualifications, timekeeping, length of service and disciplinary record). You may need to defend the mechanics of your scoring so, wherever possible, use factual data and evidence, for instance records of attendance, training and performance against KPIs.

Generally, scoring should be carried out by at least two people (e.g. appropriate management or supervisory personnel). This should remove any 'favouritism' and help ensure the scoring is as objective as possible.

TOP TIP

Do not use Last In First Out (LIFO)! What used to be the standard means of identifying staff for redundancy can now be challenged as unfair. LIFO can be discriminative and so is no longer acceptable on its own. Length of service can still be used, providing it is one of many criteria used in making the redundancy selection.

Of course, you might face a situation where a role is no longer required by the business and that role is only undertaken by one individual. In these cases, it would seem that the 'pool' and 'selection criteria' are essentially defunct. However, it is really important to examine the content of the role carefully (not just the job title), as you may find it crosses over with other roles and so a 'pool' is required after all.

Redundancy situations are never likely to be easy (even in voluntary redundancies) but the key, as always, is to maintain good communication throughout the process, starting with the need to consult with those affected.

Consultation

Consultation is a posh word for talking to people – and listening to what they have to say!

A redundancy will only be considered to be fair if the employee has been properly consulted: informed of the process, the options that may be available to them and had their chance to put forward any suggestions.

Consultation is not just a part of the process to get through as quickly as possible (during redundancy or other situations). Consultation can lead to alternatives to redundancy being identified, or at the very least, help make the process more 'human' and reduce the risk of the decision being challenged.

Very often, from the employee's point of view, it is about how they are told, how genuine the conversations are and whether they feel they have been listened to. So, take the time to consult, meet with employees and fully explain why you are having to consider making them redundant. Do all of this BEFORE you make any final decisions so that you can take what they say into consideration.

It is often said about redundancies that, 'It's not personal.' I can assure you that, for the individual on the receiving end, it is very personal and you should not forget this. What we actually mean is, 'It's not your fault that the company is having to consider making your role redundant.'

Redundancy payments

If you do make redundancies, there will generally be payments to be made. As I mentioned before these will include any payments due under the contract of employment, statutory redundancy payments and (if applicable) any enhanced redundancy payments offered by the company.

In some cases, you may decide to make further payments (e.g. a goodwill payment). If you do so, a settlement agreement might be a good means of offering this to the employee concerned. Remember that a redundancy is a dismissal and therefore can be challenged as being unfair. Therefore, even when there is a very genuine redundancy situation, a settlement agreement can help with the practicalities of making further payments to an individual while giving added peace of mind to the business.

Restructuring

There are various situations in business when you might consider having to restructure. Perhaps it comes in response to an economic need to reduce costs (labour will generally be one of your largest costs) or maybe it is the result of an assessment you make as part of your planning process. When you look at the resource you have and the resource you need for the future of your business, you may well find you have an oversupply of certain skills or that some areas of your organisation currently have more resources than others.

It is important to remember that 'restructuring' doesn't necessarily mean 'redundancy'. Of course, it can lead to this, especially if your overall need is to reduce labour costs associated with particular job functions. However, some other approaches include:

Attrition – Basically this means not replacing employees when they leave. Whether this is a good solution or not depends on the job functions being performed by leavers and whether their role can be eliminated or amalgamated into other roles without a negative impact on the business. All in all, this approach will only be appropriate if you have time to wait for employees to leave! This may be the case if employees have told you, for example, that they are looking to retire at a certain time.

Redeployment – If you find parts of your organisation have more resources than others, redeployment of staff to the area of shortage can be a good solution. This might also be appropriate when there are changes in technology or how you want a particular task to be carried out. Redeployment should, however, be approached with caution. Essentially this can involve a change in terms of employment, a change in job descriptions and possibly involve re-training.

If you have your employees' agreement to this, then you can proceed. The problem comes if you meet with resistance or if it is not practical to go ahead (e.g. the cost or the time associated with re-training is prohibitive). You might then find yourself in a position where you have unfilled positions available on one hand and redundancies on the other!

Voluntary redundancy – Another option is to start by finding out if any members of your staff are willing to take voluntary redundancy. In a similar vein to attrition situations, this will only be appropriate if the job function can be eliminated or reorganised into other roles without impacting on the essential elements of your business. Like any kind of redundancy, there will be costs to consider too. However, one problem with voluntary redundancy is that you may find you are losing the people you actually want to keep! You want to retain those people who will help you take the business forward after the restructure. You don't want all the good people taking voluntary redundancy!

There are numerous other methods of restructuring that could be deployed in your business. In some cases it might simply involve regrouping tasks into better defined jobs (going over those all important job descriptions once again) or perhaps undergoing the reorganisation of one particular department to increase efficiency. Sometimes it can be a question of offering people shorter working hours or changing your working/shift patterns to help support the needs of the business.

Remember that creating a human resources plan for your business means preparing it for the future you want it to achieve. It is important, therefore, that you consider the long-term impact of any restructuring process and what makes the best commercial solution. Before you make any decision, take into account the current labour market trends and ensure you maintain the roles you need to achieve your vision.

If you let people go now, will you face a skills shortage a few months or a year down the line?

Exits by employees...

So far, we've looked at the type of exits where the decision is generally made by the manager, rather than the employee. But, of course there are times when it is more normal for the employee to make that decision (e.g. resignation) or an exit is just a natural part of the employment life-cycle (e.g. retirement). Let's take a brief look at some best practice and processes for both of these situations.

Resignation

In the vast majority of cases, the employment relationship is ended when an employee gives notice – i.e. they tender their resignation. While this kind of exit may seem uncomplicated, there are some general areas to consider:

- Always ask the employee to confirm their resignation in writing, as this is the best way to prevent any misunderstanding.
- Acknowledge the resignation in writing, providing practical details such as notice period, return of property, leaving dates, holiday owed etc.
- The contract of employment should stipulate how much notice the employee must give. The contract should also have options for the company to consider (e.g. whether

you want the employee to work their notice or whether a payment in lieu of notice will be made).

- If the employee asks to be released without working their notice, make sure you only agree if this suits the business and confirm in writing that you will release them on the understanding that they will NOT be paid for the period of notice not worked. This may sound obvious – but it is important to clarify this in writing to avoid the possibility of any later claims!

So, let me ask a quick question: when is a resignation NOT a resignation?

Confused? Well, unfortunately there can be times when a resignation is not as straightforward as it may seem. In some cases, it may even be an indication that an employee is considering making a claim for 'constructive dismissal'. Here are two examples:

An employee resigns 'in the heat of the moment', saying something like, 'That's it! I can't work here any more. I resign!'

Accepting this as a resignation is not a safe or wise thing to do. In such instances, you may want to ask the employee to take some time to consider what they have just said, and (going back to our list above) ask them to confirm their decision in writing if they do wish to tender their resignation.

An employee confirms their resignation in writing but includes comments like 'I have no option but to resign', 'My position is untenable', or 'The actions of the company leave me no alternative'.

If the employee includes anything that indicates they are leaving because of how your company treats them, there could be trouble ahead! I would suggest you make time to discuss the comments with the employee to try to understand why they have made such statements.

These can be difficult situations to assess so, if in doubt, please take further advice!

Retirement

The final type of exit I want to talk about is retirement. An employee reaches retirement age and so their exit is arranged – simple, right?

Well, no!

While there is a defined age from which employees will be entitled to their state pension, there is no longer a 'statutory' retirement age.

In most cases, people will retire of their own free will, but some people have no desire to stop working. Aside from a few exceptions where there is a compulsory retirement related to the occupation (e.g. firefighters), you cannot insist on an employee retiring.

If you do dismiss someone just because they are of a certain age, your company would be vulnerable to a claim for unfair dismissal and age discrimination! When employers face the issue of wanting to exit an older employee who doesn't want to retire, the situation can therefore become difficult. Employers may find themselves having to commence capability or performance procedures in order to 'fairly' dismiss someone and/or entering into a settlement agreement. This is really not ideal, especially when you are dealing with someone who may have worked with you for many years.

It's good to talk!

What you can do is have a dialogue with all your employees (not just those moving towards retirement) to get an idea of their plans for the future. This can help you in so many ways, including decisions about training and development, succession planning and generally inform your HR strategy.

To sum up, there are many different situations in which you may have to deal with the exit or 'transfer' of an employee. Whether it is at the wish of the employer or employee (or both), the transfer period can be handled smoothly, providing you ensure:

- The exit fits with the commercial needs of the business.
- The legal implications are taken into account.
- The appropriate procedures are followed and active communication is maintained between all parties.

My final piece of advice is to remember that this is people we're talking about – not numbers on a spreadsheet or tools and equipment – but living, breathing people who may well find any of the exits we've discussed unwanted or stressful. So, while meeting the needs of your business must take priority, don't forget that exits should also, wherever possible, focus on helping people to move on and should be addressed with empathy.

If someone is unsuited to or unable to perform well in your company, that doesn't mean they cannot do well in another. Give them as much help as you can to assist them on their way, and both the company and the employee can come out the other end better for it.

Chapter 9 – The Coach – Training and Development

In football even the best players in the world continue to train. They have coaches and work hard with them. That's what keeps them at the top of their game.

It's the same in business. Everyone needs training and development to help them to perform and improve.

Anyone who wants to 'make it' in sport knows that success comes at a price. To compete at a high level means working hard and training hard. The rewards may be great but there are also sacrifices to be made, not least of which is the dedication that must be given to continuous training and team development.

The very same thing occurs in business.

If you want your business to 'make it', you must dedicate time to helping your people progress and develop their skills and expertise. This is done through coaching, training and professional development plans.

Before we look at what comprises good people development strategies (and how to implement them), there are two practical questions to consider:

1. Should every employee have a development plan and, if so, why?
2. Who is responsible for training and development?

Does everyone need development?

To help you answer the first of those questions, let me borrow an idea from my business coach (modelled on an extract from 'Can Your Business Step Up to the Growth Challenge?' Ray Moore, 2013).

If you had the freedom of choice (where there would be no comeback and you could recruit a replacement if you wished), how many of your team would you decide to keep?

How many of those would you keep without any changes in how they work, perform and conduct themselves?

And, how many would you keep with some changes?

If you're thinking there are some people you just wouldn't keep at all, then there is probably an issue to address. It could be anything from capability or conduct to a total mismatch of values! If you have done what you can to resolve the issue, but the problem remains, they really ought to be on your 'exit' list. A development plan is a waste of resources for these individuals, so deal with the issue (and exit) within a legal framework – as quickly as you can.

For those you would keep with some changes, think carefully about the type of changes you want to see. This should become the focus of their development plans.

For those you would keep without any changes, these are your star players. That doesn't mean you can ignore their coaching or development but rather the focus of their plans should be pitched at a level that helps your business retain and make the most of their talent.

Who is responsible for employee training and development?

This is an easy one: the responsibility for employee's training and development should be shared. That means the employee is responsible and must participate, but the business needs to provide the appropriate environment and guidance.

Every individual has to take responsibility for their own training and development. The most successful people will be the ones who look for learning opportunities in everyday activities, identify goals and activities for their own development and even prepare their own individual development plan. Their desire to succeed means they work harder, go the extra mile and are prepared to make sacrifices to achieve their ambitions. That might include putting in longer hours, taking on special projects or more responsibility, showing ongoing support to the business owner/directors, using their initiative and demonstrating (by their positive attitude) their willingness to learn.

But not everyone will have the same ambition, and people may have different ambitions at different times in their career. This is ok, and any development has to take this into consideration.

What the business needs to do (the manager/owner) is identify the areas for development, taking into consideration the individual's ambition and the needs of the business.

They must make sure everyone is pulling in the same direction. Then they have to make the important decisions about what skills need to be developed and how to play to everyone's strengths. And playing to people's strengths is important, as generally people will be more productive and positive if they are doing what they are good at or like doing. This doesn't mean that people should not try to learn new things, but some people will fundamentally be better at some things than others.

The most successful management teams will:

- Provide clear job descriptions for each employee, from which their training and development activities can be built up.
- Provide training that enables employees to meet the basic competencies for the job.
- Develop a good understanding of the knowledge, skills and abilities that the organisation will need in the future, using this to influence employee development.
- Look for everyday learning opportunities and consider each individual and how best to develop them.
- Encourage staff to be actively involved in their own development.
- Offer support to staff who identify learning activities that bring (or will bring) value to the organisation.

Training and development planning

As an SME with limited resources, it is vital that job roles and the people who fulfil those roles are aligned with the needs of your business – essentially this is 'good' HR and you cannot afford for things to be otherwise. Training and development should be aligned with the needs of the business too.

The first question therefore is:

What does the business need from its people?

Generally, if you've already gone through the processes of assessing and creating the job roles your organisation needs, then the answer to this is simple. Most SMEs **need** every one of their employees to carry out their role and duties at the optimum level while being flexible to the changing demands of the business.

Basic training

I would be surprised if your business (and each role you have within it) has no basic or mandatory training. It may be quite generic like IT systems within your organisation, specific company procedures, product or service knowledge, or specific industry requirements for a particular qualification. At the very least, you should have essential induction training, which helps new employees to settle in and become effective at their jobs quickly.

There are probably some very common elements to your induction: things that every new employee needs to know. If this is the case, the best thing to do is to have a standard induction process that you can repeat for each new starter. Some ideas would be to have an induction booklet that employees can work through to 'check-off' that they have covered certain areas, provided required documentation and received required information from you. You can have a PowerPoint presentation or a video to explain what the company does, its key standards and/or mission statement. Where possible, give people access to the information they need, and allow them to review this at their own pace and check things off as they progress. Managers can then review this with the new starter at regular intervals.

Another positive way to help induct new people is to assign a 'buddy' to help show them the ropes. But be sure this is someone who is positive and who will communicate the rules and standards (and generally how you do things) in the right way. It will take a new starter a few months to really settle in and get to know the business. A good induction will help speed this along.

Further training and development

After this, the best approach is to create a training and development plan for each individual that focuses on building up their skills and abilities so they can be more effective at their job role and become a more valuable asset to the company.

In some cases, you may think it is very clear what skills and development are needed for a particular member of staff, but it is generally more effective if you prepare any plans together, allowing the employee to contribute. This way you are more likely to get their buy-in, resulting in raised levels of engagement from the employee and bringing the positive return on investment your company needs.

Although it is better to eventually have formal written down plans, ideas for staff development may well come from more informal discussions and suggestions made by your employees. A good example might be a situation where you are discussing how to improve a product or service with an employee. Perhaps it becomes clear that certain skills or knowledge may be needed and therefore, as a natural outcome, a training and development opportunity arises!

Taking marketing as an example, how many organisations in recent years have identified a need to use social media? How have they done this? Well, they all had to develop their understanding and knowledge of social media – maybe with external support or not! Those individuals who now deliver the marketing messages via social media had to learn and develop their skills in order to meet the needs of the business.

Training and development methods

So much has changed in our world that, in many ways, the decisions we have to make can seem overwhelming. Once upon a time, training and development at work probably meant being taken onto some kind of Apprenticeship or Internship programme where the training was largely 'on-the-job' – personal instructions passed down from supervisors to employees with possibly some classroom based learning too.

Nowadays, we may no longer have the 'job for life' but we do have a much greater belief in the idea of 'lifelong learning'. Coupled with the impact of advances in technology, there is now a huge range of learning activities and opportunities to choose from. It's no surprise that many SMEs find the task of selecting appropriate training/development methods for each of their employees a burden; many just don't know where to start. This is why I believe it is important for each individual employee to be involved in identifying the best means of achieving their development goals themselves.

Different approaches will work for different people and, even for the same employee, different methods may work better at different times or stages of their career.

The point I'm trying to make is that, while a variety of training methods can be used, the key is always to ensure the learning experience is appropriate to the need – taking into account what works for the organisation, the role and the stage of development your employee is working at.

Sending your employees on training courses or classroom-based activities may be an effective method at times, but it is not the only solution to upgrading skills or performance (and it is normally quite an expensive option). There are numerous other approaches you could take, many of which are cost-effective. Some rely only on the everyday activities taking place at your company, alongside a commitment from your employees to be open to what they can learn from the things going on around them.

Here are some of the methods you and your team might consider:

College or university courses

Sponsoring a member of staff to study at this level requires strong commitment from all sides, but can be a great way of motivating an employee while injecting the latest academic knowledge into your organisation.

The good news is that most professional level courses will require the student to attend 'class' occasionally with the majority of reading/study expected to be carried out at home (thus causing minimal disruption to the business).

TOP TIP

You may want to have a Training Agreement in place for any training where you are contributing financially. As well as stating the employee's obligations around the training, these can allow you to require an employee to repay the cost to the company should they leave shortly after you have invested in their development – something that a lot of SMEs find frustrating! (See more in Chapter 4.)

Courses, seminars or workshops

While these generally present a formal training opportunity, you still have a choice about how you actually implement them. You might send staff off-site for the day or arrange for a facilitator to work internally within your organisation.

Interactive technology based learning

From online training courses to webinars and podcasts, the technology we live with today offers learning opportunities that cover every topic imaginable!

While choosing from the profusion of opportunities out there may be difficult, if you can stay focused on the skill level required for the role, there is much to gain from this approach. There may be some cost involved but the trade-off is that generally this kind of learning is carried out by the individual in their own time. Even if the activity is undertaken during work time, the employee does not have to leave the office and so the time commitment and associated expenses are both reduced.

There is also a wealth of **free resources** out there. You can find 'how to' do almost anything just by looking at YouTube! Other free online tools can help with a wide range of skills – for instance, learning to 'touch type', training on Excel or other software, or even information about how to work out VAT!

Books

Old-fashioned? Never!

Books remain an effective means of meeting all kinds of training and development needs. You might bring in textbooks to help staff with technical training or specific functions of their job. Management or personal development books are useful for managers and those aspiring to move into management positions – and can help promote a particular style of leadership or culture for the company.

Another time saving option is to provide audiobooks. That way, employees can listen to them during their journey to work, on the treadmill or at home!

Let's not forget – you are reading (or listening) to a book right now!

Reading

Didn't we just say books? Well, reading doesn't stop there! Information and knowledge can be found everywhere – in industry magazines, news coverage, blogs and much more.

Making sure you and your team are 'plugged-in' to these resources (receiving regular updates on relevant topics) is a great way of keeping up-to-date with the latest news and trends in your industry. This can be an invaluable part of ongoing personal development.

Individual coaching

The great thing about coaching arrangements is that they encourage individuals to become more accountable for their own development.

Coaching is about helping individuals find the answers for themselves. It may involve an experienced manager offering support, advice, guidance and feedback to a less experienced employee. Alternatively, coaching may be provided by an external coach.

The secret is to find the right coach for the situation and the individual.

Peer-to-peer learning

There are many ways in which you can facilitate an environment where employees learn from each other.

For instance, you might make it part of your strategy that those who attend formal training do so on the condition that they help to cascade their knowledge/skill to others within the organisation.

Other ideas include job shadowing, where an employee observes another person at their work. Such activity can result in people gaining a better appreciation of how different roles work together for the benefit of the company.

Another option is peer-assisted learning where two employees with different areas of expertise agree to help each other learn tasks that will bring about an improvement in their performance.

And then there is the buddy system – often used with new-starters – where a work colleague will support a new employee, guide them through and 'teach them the job'.

Joining in!

Attending a professional conference, networking or sitting on a committee or panel associated with your industry... all of these can be great ways of meeting and learning from others (while expanding your business contacts).

As well as improving confidence, participation in such activities can help people to understand different perspectives, widen their knowledge base and perform better at their role. It can also be a great way of opening your company up to new and interesting ideas.

Stretching

I'm not talking about the footballers again here!
'Stretching' involves giving an employee a task that has previously been outside of their general duties or pitched at a level above their current position.

For example, you might ask an employee to chair a meeting (if they have not done this before) or you might give them a special project.

There are many more options you could consider. Remember that the better trained your team are the better they can perform, and that has a direct impact on the bottom line of your business. As Richard Branson said:

'Train your people well enough so they can leave, treat them well enough so they don't want to.'

What about you...

It is very easy to forget that we all need development – even those of us who are in management positions or are 'the Boss'. In some ways our own development is even more important as this can help us become better managers and business owners, something that can greatly benefit the company and everyone who works there!

Many SMEs start their businesses because they are good at what they do and have a belief that they can do it better or differently. I include myself in this. I had been in HR for many years when I decided I wanted to do it differently! I wanted to work specifically for SMEs as they generally had no HR departments to call on... and I wanted to make HR easier for SMEs.

However, while I had lots of knowledge, experience and qualifications around HR and employment law, I had very little (if any) around running a business. A few years into running my company; Practical HR, I started to realise this and to feel quite vulnerable. My solution was to get some coaching and start learning how to run a business; the coaching I received was invaluable.

Don't get me wrong, I am still learning and I am sure this will never stop (every day's a school day!), but I do know much more now and can see how this has helped me develop my business.

So, first of all, I'd like to say thank you to my coach! Secondly, I would like to encourage any manager or business owner out there to not only invest in their team but also to invest in themselves and their own development.

Never stop learning

We live in an ever-changing world and, if we stand still, we actually end up going backwards! You cannot stand still in business, which means you have to keep learning and so do your employees.

Chapter 10 – Don't Let HR Hold You Back

In football no successful team ever let anything or anyone hold them back. They continually adapt, refine the team and improve their game plan. They know what their goal is.

Having worked with SMEs for many years, I cannot emphasise enough how important it is to get that HR foundation right.

I have seen numerous situations that have arisen that have caused frustration, taken up valuable management time and cost money. In the majority of cases, issues could have been avoided or dealt with more quickly (and amicably) had there been a solid HR foundation.

There will always be HR issues in a business, because you are dealing with people, but it's about being able to minimize these and the disruption to the business.

I also appreciate that, for an SME, HR is often not a priority... until it becomes a priority! Save yourself the worry and money that can come from not having good HR and get your foundation in place. And it's not just good for you, it's good for your business and the people who work in your business.

Over the years I have heard many business owners talk about how they have downsized their business *because* they did not want to have to deal with the HR issues. How sad is this? Not just for the business owner, but for the people in the business and even the economy as a whole - with all the lost opportunity and business growth that never happened.

As I said at the start of this book, I don't want any business to be held back because of HR and employment law. And it doesn't have to be that way if you take a pro-active approach. So in this final chapter, let me just summarise the key things that make up the HR foundation one more time. And don't forget, there are people who can help you with this. You do not have to go it alone, but the longer you put it off, the longer it will take to introduce.

So here are the steps again that will guide you to a solid HR foundation... and beyond.

3 steps to the HR foundation

Here are the 3 steps to your HR foundation:

1. Contracts of employment
2. HR policies & procedures, codes of conduct and standards
3. Implementation and consistency

Step 1 – Contracts of Employment

Good contracts of employment will give you protection and flexibility. They will support what you need to do in any situation (or get it wrong, and they will restrict you).

Make sure your contracts give you the options you may need in any situation. This means going beyond the basic legal requirements of providing written terms, and taking time to consider what is needed now for the business and what may be needed in the future. Remember, contracts are also communication documents so they should be written in plain English.

Step 2 - HR policies & procedures, codes of conduct and standards

Along with your contracts, your policies & procedures, codes of conduct and standards will set out your rules and how you want things to be done. They will help managers manage and set expectations with your employees and, if enforced fairly and consistently, will built trust and co-operation.

Without these in place you will be limited in what action you can take in any situation and/or find yourself facing disputes and needless HR issues.

Step 3 – Implementation and consistency

Apply your rules consistently and address 'rule-breaking' quickly. HR problems will not go away. If they are not addressed, they will fester and take longer to deal with.

Remember that people like boundaries. They like to know where they stand. This will give security and, applied consistently, will even support the wellbeing of your people.

The majority of people will play by the rules if they know what they are. And for the minority who don't, having your rules in writing (and clearly communicated) will allow you to deal with any matters more quickly (and amicably).

Communication

Don't forget one of the most important elements – communication. It may sound obvious, but I've seen a lot of SMEs put a lot of time and effort into drafting their rules and then fail to communicate them effectively... and also fail to then keep them up to date.

An employee handbook that sits on a shelf gathering dust is not effective communication. Nor is running through the handbook at speed during the induction process in order to 'tick a box'.

People need to be reminded on an ongoing basis and need ongoing access to the rules. After a while they will become part of the culture and you will find that your people self-manage. But this will only happen if rules are clear and applied consistently.

Rules will change. This may be employment law changing or it may be internal rules that need to change because of changes in the business. That's ok, just make sure you communicate any changes and give people time to adjust. This will generally mean having to remind people (enforcing the new rule) a few times. This is not because they are deliberately breaking the new rule, it's because they need to build a new habit!

Beyond the foundation

Once your rules are in place, they set a standard for everything else you do. They allow you to recruit more easily, manage more easily and exit more easily.

Recruitment

With recruitment you need to be clear about what you want someone to do – the job description. And you need to know the type of personal attributes, experience and qualifications the person will need – the person specification.

Communicate these at an early stage to candidates so they can make an informed decision about whether they think the role is right for them.

When someone joins, make sure you induct them well. A good induction will help them settle in more easily and allow them to contribute more quickly.

During employment

With a good job description in place from the outset, people will have a much clearer idea about what is expected of them. If job descriptions include measurement and performance indicators, they will allow employees and you to monitor progress more easily. This means that if there are problems these can be addressed sooner rather than later. This gives everyone the opportunity to 'fix' any problems. This may mean more support and/or training to help them in the early days. Remember we are all different. Some people will pick things up very quickly, others will take more time, but once they have it, they have it!

Invest in your people at an early stage (and on an ongoing basis) and it will be to the benefit of the business and the individual.

Let people know and understand how they contribute and add value. This will give them more purpose and people with a purpose perform to a higher standard.

Develop your people

We all need training and development if we want to grow as individuals. In the workplace this can help people do their job better, increase their self-confidence and personal wellbeing. We all like to feel as if we are achieving and moving forward, and training and development is one way to help achieve this. Development can take many forms: online courses, reading, going to college/university, learning from your peers and on the job etc. And over time will probably be a combination of all of these.

You cannot teach someone if they do not want to learn, and this is why development is a joint responsibility. The business needs to provide the environment and opportunity. The individual needs to engage with this.

The end of employment

Not everyone will stay. Some will leave of their own accord, others because you help them!

If someone is not right for your business – it may be they are unable to do the job, or they have the wrong attitude – help them move on as quickly as possible. A 'bad apple' will have a negative impact on the entire team. The team will also be looking to see what you are doing about it!

Where you can support someone, then do. But if it's not going to work out, deal with it. If you can help someone move on positively then do so. Sometimes an honest conversation is what's needed. And remember, just because someone is not right for your business, this does not mean they will not be successful in another.

In a minority of cases you may have to deal with serious misconduct. Deal with it swiftly. You cannot help these people move on in a positive way, but you do need to exit them from your business.

Conclusion

Running a business and employing people is not easy. There are many challenges along the way.

But ultimately, your business is only as good as your people. The better your people perform, the better your business will perform. This simple fact on its own means that an investment in HR has to add value.

It can be frustrating and demoralising when you have an HR problem. But it can be exhilarating and exciting when you have a team of people who are all pulling in the same direction and achieving for the business.

It's worth the investment to get your HR foundation in place. It's worth it for you, your business and your people.

Free Resources

www.yourhr.guide is an online HR guide for SMEs with general guidance on the most common issues facing them, plus 'how to' information and over 150 templates including letters, HR policies, forms and employment contracts.

You can access the free resources referred to throughout this book and many more by visiting www.yourhr.guide.

These include:

- Written Statement of Terms (what the law says you must issue to your employees and workers)
- Example new starter checklist
- Example leaver's checklist
- Example job description
- Example person specification
- Example Standards Policy

Other websites

www.practicalhr.co.uk

The Practical HR main website providing a summary of services and products available.

www.yourhr.space

An online HR platform that supports and communicates your HR foundation, with HR experts who work with you to draft and maintain all your documents

Other support services

Advisory, Conciliation and Arbitration Service (ACAS)

ACAS is a government organisation that provides a free helpline for employers and employees. Their website sets out quite clearly what they do:

'We provide information, advice, training, conciliation and other services for employers and employees to help prevent or resolve workplace problems.'

You can visit the ACAS website at www.acas.org.uk.

Book references

Ray Moore – 'The Levels'

Jim Collins – 'Good to Great'

Jack Welch – 'Winning'

About the Author

Paula Fisher started her career in HR at the age of 18 when she joined the Marks and Spencer's young management training scheme. After five years with M&S she went on to work in other blue chip organisations such as Burberry and Matalan, holding HR management and senior management positions.

She then left the corporate world and commenced a Law degree (as a very mature student!) at Anglia Ruskin University, graduating in 1997 with a First-Class Honours degree. She formed her first business, with a business partner (providing HR services to SMEs) in the 3rd year of her Law degree. After five years, she left this business to pursue her academic studies and completed her Master's degree in Law and Employment Relations.

In 2002 Paula founded Practical HR Ltd, literally working from her spare bedroom. For the first two years she subsidised the business by teaching Employment Law on the CIPD course (Certificate in Personnel and Development) at Anglia Ruskin Business School.

Practical HR was, and still is, focused on providing pragmatic and commercial support to SMEs. In addition to traditional consultancy services, Paula has created a number of online solutions, recognising that HR can be supported by technology. This has culminated in the development of YourHR.space, an online portal that solves the HR compliance and communication problem for SMEs. This was developed as a direct result of Paula identifying the common problem that SMEs have in keeping up to date with HR and employment law, and communicating information to employees.

Practical HR is located in Essex, just outside Southend-on-Sea. Here, Paula works with a small, dedicated team who all share the same passion for providing practical solutions and great customer services. All the team are dedicated to making HR easier for clients and they continue to innovate to achieve this.

Practical HR also has a second office based near Bishop's Stortford, on a wide beam canal boat! This office is used for meetings with local clients and as a place where Paula goes to focus on writing, drafting or to concentrate on product development. A boat on the river is an ideal spot for tranquillity and inspiration.

Paula is married to Peter Fisher. They met at school (many, many years ago) and will soon be celebrating their 30th wedding anniversary. They live in a small village in Essex. Paula's spare time is spent walking her dogs, gardening and enjoying good food, good wine (and the occasional gin and tonic) and good times with friends.

Paula and Peter enjoy travelling and aim to spend more time doing this in the coming years. Since discovering the Prosecco region in Italy (yes, there really is one) they are keen to explore other wine regions. Champagne is high on the list!

You can contact Paula via email on paula@practicalhr.co.uk or find her on LinkedIn.